# NORTHERN MISTS

# NORTHERN MISTS
## Carl O. Sauer

University of California Press
Berkeley and Los Angeles

University of California Press
Berkeley & Los Angeles

Cambridge University Press
London, England

# CONTENTS

# MAPS

# CHAPTER I THE WESTERING OF EUROPE IN THE MIDDLE AGES

*PERSPECTIVE*

Columbus returned from Española in the spring of 1493 to report that he had found the Indies. Peter Martyr, observing at court the exhibit of strange people and products, thought that Columbus had reached, instead of the Indies, the island of Antilia. At the time, Antilia was thought to be a great island lying far out to sea to the west of Portugal. It was thus shown in somewhat detailed outline on an Italian chart of 1424, which has recently been discovered and interpreted by Armando Cortesão.[1] In similar configuration and location it appeared on map after map of the fifteenth century under that name, which may be of Portuguese origin. The time was one of strongly emergent interest in the western ocean and in its extension to the south. Cartography flourished and globes as well as maps were being made. Where knowledge failed, legend supplied islands to be placed upon the expanse of sea, especially to the west. The legend of Antilia may be late, perhaps of the fifteenth century. Other legendary islands, notably those of the Seven Cities, Brasil, Yma, and Saint Brendan, are of greater age. The Middle Ages held the Ocean Sea to be strewn with islands, largely wondrous. Those who lived on its borders turned their attention and imagination to the west.

The theme proposed here is the faring out to sea during the Middle Ages from Atlantic Europe. Some of the lore is

[1] *The Nautical Chart of 1424* (Coimbra, 1954).

1

of voyages of adventure in strange parts, which blend ancient myth with partly remembered events. Sagas told of real persons who got to places that may perhaps be identified today. Chronicles and geographies set down soberly what had been seen and experienced. In time, official records added their documentation. By the fifteenth century, the nature and extent of European seafaring becomes legible in major outline. The mists of time before then are broken by less certain vistas.

Throughout the Middle Ages, men took ships onto the high seas with confidence. It was not the "tenebrous sea" of antiquity but an invitation to open horizons where one might find new fishing or sea hunting, distant commerce, land to live in, adventure and combat, or peace and solitude. The incentives varied with the people who went out at different times in widening reconnaissance of the western ocean. Atlantic Europe acquired increasing and largely shared familiarity with a wide reach of sea to the west, its seasons, winds, currents, and life.

## IN NORTHERN MISTS

In 1911 Fridtjof Nansen published a two-volume work called *In Northern Mists*; the title of the present volume is borrowed from that work.[2] Others before and after him have written on European exploration of the North Atlantic Ocean. His work is still the classic in this field. As he was conversant with what had been learned before him, so must later students acknowledge their obligation to him. As explorer of the Arctic, he had widest experience of its physical nature and life and of its approaches from Europe. Nansen applied his observations to intimate study of the old Norse

[2] Fridtjof Nansen, *In Northern Mists* (London, 1911). Nansen's bibliography is inclusive to 1911, and the index is excellent. Richard Hennig, *Terrae Incognitae*, vols. 2 and 3 (Leiden, 1953 and 1956), continued the bibliography to midcentury; useful, with caution.

literature and other medieval sources. These source materials he formed into an historical geography, using many and lengthy excerpts and translations, which I have used freely.

Nansen was never ill-informed or inattentive. He has been called hypercritical, as of the Vinland voyages. Archaeology has since added to knowledge of Greenland and the spread of the Eskimos, but the work of Nansen remains the most balanced and insightful study of the northern seas during the Middle Ages. It extends beyond the central theme that limits the present topic but is fundamental to it and is so accepted. I have given more attention to somewhat lower latitudes and to peoples other than Norse, but the title chosen by the old master still holds, as does much of his overall view.

## FACING THE WESTERN OCEAN

To the people living about the Mediterranean Sea, Atlantic Europe was the farthest back country. The Romans, for example, viewed it as the land of barbarians who kept breaking the peace and who inhabited the shores of a dif-

Mermaid, from *Flateyjarbok* (Nansen).

3

ficult and repellent sea, *mare tenebrosum*. However, to the natives of its shores, Celts and Basques and Germanic peoples, the sea was the frontier of opportunity to provide food, to build and man vessels in which to go out, and to move to new homes.

The outline of the western sea as here concerned may be drawn roughly. The European frontage extends from North Cape to Cape Finisterre, Portugal being somewhat marginal. Its western shores extend from southwest Greenland to New England. To the north is the Arctic Ocean, where the open sea gives way to pack ice and frozen surface, a widely shifting cold barrier well to the north of Scandinavia but one which may be encountered down the entire east coast of Greenland. At the south there is wide passage from the northern waters to the calm and sunny seas beneath the persistent air mass of the Bermuda High, known to sailors as the Horse Latitudes. Here the Azores Islands lie, midway between Portugal and Newfoundland, well placed for voyaging northwest. By convention of cartography, the North Atlantic Ocean reaches south to the Equator. Nansen's sea of northern mists, with which alone we are concerned, is its northern part, unnamed except for the bordering seas. It will be referred to as the Northern Atlantic (map 1).

Across this ocean the general circulation of the atmosphere entrains an eastward procession of polar air masses, bringing frequent changes of weather, cloudy, stormy, and fair. Winds may continue out of a westerly quarter for days or weeks. The circulation of air powers a northeastward drift of warm surface water that begins as the Gulf Stream and reaches all the ocean coast of Europe. Fogbanks are notorious in season. They form where warm air meets cold air or water, especially along shore, and are most common and persistent off Newfoundland in summer. The likeliest season for clear skies is in fall and early winter, a knowledge

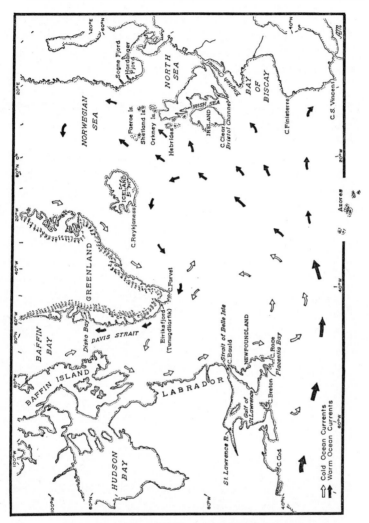

Map 1. The Northern Atlantic Ocean.

that seafarers used to their advantage. They might encounter headwinds at any season as they sailed west or be storm-driven far off course, but they expected favoring winds again.

5

Knowing the hazards and moods of their sea was part of their basic learning, reading the signs of sky, water, bird flight.

## SUSTENANCE FROM THE SEA

This northern sea is extraordinarily rich in life, both in quantity and diversity. Streams contribute to it mineral and organic nutrients from the greater part of North America and a large part of Europe. This great aquarium is kept stirred, mixed, and aerated by current, wind, and tide, within temperatures, salinities, and insolation favorable to organic reproduction. Masses of plant and animal plankton, "the pastures of the sea," support vast numbers of surface-feeding fish, such as herring and mackerel, and in shoal waters bottom-feeding flat fish. Game fish, cod and its relatives, prey upon the smaller fish. Sea fowl and seals hunt the coastal waters and breed in rookeries on shore. Until recently, right whales ranged the plankton beds for small crustaceans. Shoals in these northern waters may be more productive than is the land. It has been estimated that the English Channel produces annually thirteen tons of organic matter per hectare, which is about twice the yield of a good meadow in a good year in those parts.[3] And the food available to man from the sea furnishes him protein and fats.

Immemorial sea fishing and hunting grounds extend along the mainland from the Lofoten Islands off northern Norway to the Bay of Biscay and all about the British Isles. The banks of the North Sea came to be fished during the Middle Ages. The Faeroe Islands, Iceland, and Greenland were occupied by settlers who depended largely on the resources of the sea. Last of all, the newfound northern lands across the ocean were taken under exploitation by Europeans for their wealth of fish.

Fishing and hunting at sea vary locally with the time

[3] Fritz Bartz, *Die Grossen Fischereiräume* (Wiesbaden, 1964), I, 12.

of year but are likely to be productive at all seasons. Nor are they subject to the vicissitudes of weather that affect husbandry in higher latitudes. In parts better favored by climate and soil, the sea supplemented the income of farmer and herdsman and gave subsistence to landless and poor folk. Where soil was meager and season of plant growth brief and uncertain, as in much of the more northern countries, the sea and its coasts gave major sustenance. In some parts of the farther north, European civilization was established without any tillage, and animal husbandry became subordinate to the largess of the sea. The ability to take to the sea determined whether men thrived or even survived.

South of Cape Finisterre the sea is warmer and less productive. Cod, herring, and mackerel of the colder waters are replaced by sardines, anchovies, and tunnies. Right whales rarely strayed south beyond the Bay of Biscay. The supplement of sea food still is important to the Portuguese diet, partly from local inshore fishing and partly from *bacalhao*, as they call the dried cod their fishermen have taken from the banks of Newfoundland since about the end of the fifteenth century. This seemingly sudden extension of Portuguese fishing from home shores across the sea to American waters by annual fishing parties still poses a problem. It underscores the marginal maritime position of Portugal, with a narrow and limited resource of sea food along shore and a near desert sea to the south, the Azores giving entry into northwestern waters of rich yield. Portugal and the Azores, toward the southern fringe of the North Atlantic circulation of air and sea, took an important part in opening higher latitudes of the western ocean.

## THE SHIFT FROM MEDITERRANEAN DOMINANCE

Medieval Europe underwent a shift in dominance from Mediterranean to Atlantic lands. The former Roman provinces of the west, largely of Romanized Celts overrun by Germanic tribes, took form as nation-states. Christianity penetrated to the northern frontiers of Rome, all along the Rhine and across the Channel into England. In the fifth century it won by rapid and peaceful conversion Celtic Ireland, which had remained beyond the Roman realm. In the Germanic north the acceptance of Christianity was not completed until the end of the tenth century. The civilizing influence of Christianity found expressions of its own in the west, in Gothic building, a monasticism of service that spread from Ireland to the continent, the cultivation of native language and letters, the nurture of the arts and practical crafts. Industries developed and commerce by land and sea supported the growth of cities peopled by free townsmen.

Meanwhile time was running against the Mediterranean lands. The Muslim advance along the eastern and southern coasts reduced the supply of food from those parts and gradually blocked the great commerce with the East that had brought wealth to Italian cities. Less attention has been given to the low yield of food of the Mediterranean Sea and to the declining productivity of much of its land. The great alluvial valleys of the Nile and Po are of unsurpassed fertility, which is maintained by irrigation in the former and by drainage in the latter. The Mediterranean uplands, on the other hand, have been subject to long depletion. Largely they are limestone lands, fertile but susceptible to soil erosion. They have been plowed overlong, to grow wheat and barley, overgrazed, and depleted of trees. The whole length of the Mediterranean is scarred by man's wastage of the soil, here by gullies, there by the mineral color of subsoil from which the topsoil has been stripped. A secondary scrub vegetation has colonized the wasted surfaces. Maquis, garrigue, heath, and stands of palmetto mask surfaces that once were tilled fields and pastures. Resinous scent of leaf, colorful bloom of rock rose, broom, and heather are present reminders of lost fertility.

The ancient Greeks knew that their land was declining in fertility. The loss continued and accelerated in the time of medieval commerce. Where Venice, the greatest commercial state, ruled, the devastation may be extreme, as throughout the Dalmatian coast, or severe, as in the Ionian and Aegean islands. The splendid old cities of Tuscany are in the midst of a land of exposed red subsoil and of stream beds filled with sediment. An old proverb about Genoa begins "a sea without fish, mountains without forests."

Mediterranean lands produced less and less. The Mediterranean Sea, almost tideless and fed by few rivers, is of low productivity. Its fishermen are poor, few, and get a small and indifferent catch. Fishing improves markedly west of the Strait of Gibraltar, although this is not one of the better parts of the Atlantic.

With shrinking prospects at home Italians and also Catalans turned increasingly to service abroad. Italian banking houses established branches in the west. By the fifteenth century Italian factors and agents were resident in number in the major Atlantic port cities, from Sevilla and Lisbon to London and Bristol. Italy was still the center of communication for news and finance and provided venture capital and persons of experience for enterprises in the western countries. The economic initiative shifted to new directions and places; the Mediterranean had become subordinate to a Europe fronting on the Atlantic.

## NOTES ON COMMERCIAL AND POLITICAL GEOGRAPHY OF THE FIFTEENTH CENTURY

The intent here is to follow European seafaring in northern waters back through the Middle Ages, from the familiar late fifteenth century to the dim times of the sixth

9

century. To the Portuguese, the fifteenth is the start of modern history; by our equally self-centered calendar, time is reckoned as before or after Columbus. The beginning fifteenth century as a whole was one of accelerating action on land and sea, of changing scene and participants.

The northern part of the stage centered on the southern part of the North Sea, on the coast from Hamburg and Bremen by way of Holland and Flanders to London. Flanders was the leading entrepôt of Atlantic Europe, Bruges the great center of commerce, Ghent and Ypres the producers of wool and linen cloth for large and profitable export. The Flemish burghers bought raw materials, fabricated them, marketed finished goods, and financed commerce. Mainly they left the carriage to others. In the early part of the fifteenth century Hanseatic merchantmen trafficked all about the North, Norwegian, and Baltic seas, loading grain, wool, hides, pelts, naval stores, fish. They built and manned stout cargo ships, such as the broad-beamed cogs (*Koggen*), capacious and seaworthy in rough waters. The Hanseatic trade was well organized and ranged from Novgorod and Visby in the east to Iceland, including major counters (ware and counting houses) in Flanders and England. Unlike the merchants of Flanders, those of the Hanse operated a large merchant fleet, but were little interested in going beyond the familiar northern seas and commodities.

With the growth of nation-states in northern Europe the power of the Hanse declined and trade passed largely to the Dutch of Zeeland and Holland. In the course of the century these became successful merchants at sea, mariners, and shipbuilders. Dutch seafaring, however, did not extend beyond North European waters until well into the sixteenth century.

England and France were engaged in the Hundred Years' War to midcentury. The last major battle was in

1453, when the English were defeated at Castillon-en-Dordogne to the east of Bordeaux. The war on land was fought in the north and southwest of France, which was badly ravaged and largely lost the use of its ports. Although England lost all of its holdings in France except Calais, English shipping was little affected, except for the Channel ports. Bristol in particular, protected to the south by the Cornish peninsula, flourished. It had superior fishing grounds to the west and a privileged position in trade with Ireland, and early in the century it began sending ships to Iceland. Bristol ships traded to Portugal, Madeira, and the Azores. Bristol therefore will require attention as a major gateway into the Atlantic.

Situated south of the battleground of Aquitaine, the Spanish Basque coast and adjacent Asturias were important on the high seas. And most important of all was the coast of Portugal. From the southwest cape of Europe, St. Vincent, Prince Henry began to probe the Atlantic and opened the age of maritime exploration.

# CHAPTER II   THE PORTUGUESE AT SEA

*BEFORE PRINCE HENRY*

The sixteenth-century Portuguese historian João de Barros wrote that before the time of Prince Henry the Navigator "the Portuguese were not accustomed to venture far into the open sea, and all their navigating was limited to daytime sailing in sight of the land." The oft-cited statement is less than adequate.

The Portuguese were a nation of farmers (*lavradores*) and fishermen of coastal waters, frugal and industrious as they still are, living as a small nation of very modest resources, and united in resistance to their aggressive neighbor Castile. As the southwestern headland of Europe Portugal was also, particularly at Lisbon, the medieval meeting place of the water-borne commerce of the Mediterranean and northwest Europe. The former was mainly Italian, largely carried by galleys. From the north, English trading ships visited Lisbon and Porto well before the fifteenth century.

Portuguese kings had the wit to see the advantage of their maritime location and to undertake to turn Portugal to the Atlantic. The beginning was made by King Dinis, called *El Rei Lavrador* because he encouraged good farming. He was also the first royal forester of Europe, and made extensive plantings of pines (*Pinus pinaster*) for timber and naval stores. These still grace the sandy coastal plain about Leiria. In 1284 he entered into a trade pact with England, which was followed by a treaty of defense. In 1317 he named a Genoese merchant, Manuel Pessagno, as hereditary admiral, to have always with him twenty men from Genoa, experts on the sea, to act as masters and pilots.[1]

Italian interest, most particularly at Genoa, turned to the western ocean as trade routes through the Levant became blocked by Muslim power. Perhaps a sea route south around Africa would lead to India. In 1291, the Vivaldi brothers of Genoa passed through the Strait of Gibraltar to make such attempt, it is thought. They were last heard of at Cape Juby across from the Canary Islands. In 1312(?) a Genoese ship found the eastern Canary Islands. A temporary settlement was made on the island of Lanzarote, which still bears the name of its discoverer.[2] Independent Genoese explorations in the Atlantic, the presence of Genoese mariners and merchants in Portugal, and their employment by King Dinis to train the Portuguese in seamanship, were first steps that initiated the great period of Portuguese oceanic discovery.

Alfonso IV succeeded to the throne in 1325 and directed his attention south, in particular to the Canary Islands, sending ships under command of Italian officers and largely with Italian crews. One of these voyages resulted in the first description of the Canaries, attributed to Boccaccio, reporting on the first sea voyage undertaken by the Portuguese Crown (1341?).[3] Further ventures at sea were stopped by a war with Castile and later in the century by an outbreak of the Black Death.

Italian seamen continued to teach navigation of the high seas to the Portuguese. Italian merchants settled in increasing numbers in Lisbon and Porto as their Levant trade fell off. Portugal's repeated wars with Castile brought English support at arms. In 1385 King John I of Portugal, with the aid of English bowmen, inflicted a disastrous defeat on the

---

[1] A. Cortesão, p. 52.
[2] See Hennig, vol. 3, chs. 130 and 134, for a résumé of the Vivaldi and Lanzarote voyages.
[3] A. Cortesão, p. 50, and Hennig, vol. 3, ch. 243.

attacking Castilian troops at Aljubarrota. This was followed in 1386 by the Treaty of Windsor, permanently allying Portugal and England, and in 1387 by the marriage of John I and Philippa of Lancaster, daughter of John of Gaunt. Five sons, including Prince Henry the Navigator, and a daughter were born of the union. The daughter, Isabel, married Philip the Good of Burgundy and thus brought closer ties with Flanders. Besides the English seamen and merchants in Portuguese ports there was a strong English influence at court. The end of the century saw Portugal strongly bound to England and Flanders, ready to enter on its great enterprise overseas.

The battleground of Aljubarrota is marked by the national shrine of the monastery of Santa María da Batalha, the noblest Gothic structure in Portugal, begun in 1388. Its blending of English and Flemish architecture with Portuguese and Moorish elements shows the link between Portugal and northern lands. King John, his English queen, and Prince Henry are buried in the chapel. The site of the battle, between Coimbra and Lisbon, tells how close Castile came to the conquest of the country. The great and affecting monument declares Portugal as part of an Atlantic community, started on its course into world affairs. Prince Henry was born while the building was under way.

## PRINCE HENRY AND THE AZORES

Prince Henry the Navigator (1394–1460) made Portugal a maritime nation. To do so he used up his own fortune and a good part of that of the Order of Christ of which he was Grand Master. Beginning in 1416, he sent expeditions south along the desert shores of Africa without notable results until Cape Blanco, beyond the Canary Islands, was reached in 1441. The uninhabited Madeira Islands had been known casually to Spanish and other ships returning from the Canaries but were "discovered" by the Portuguese in 1419 and colonized somewhat later (1426?). Their date of settlement is obscure, partly because a Portuguese party set fire to the wholly forested main island. The fire is said to have burned for seven years, destroying the forests that had given the islands their name. The occupation of the Madeira group gave an excellently placed ocean base for provisioning ships going south. Also it was the first and highly successful plantation of Portuguese colonists overseas, producing sugar and wine.

About 1420 Henry chose windswept Cape St. Vincent, southwesternmost headland of Europe, to be his seat. In this remote place, peopled by fishermen and shepherds, he built Sagres, with an astronomical observatory, a naval training school, and an institute and library of cosmography. Here he assembled able mathematicians, astronomers, mapmakers, cosmographers, drawing especially on Jewish and Arab scholars. He spent much of his time there, conferring with scholars and navigators and planning the course of maritime discovery.

At about the time that Henry was organizing his marine institute at Sagres, his brother Pedro started on a nine-year journey through European countries, including a stay at the Danish court. Danish knowledge of the northern sea was thus taken to Portugal. An extraordinary royal family this, in which two princes spent their youth acquiring geographical knowledge.

Portuguese scholars like to think of Prince Henry as forming the grand design of a sea route to the Indies early in his life. Others have denied this, stressing his activity as a crusader or attributing to him interest in African slave and gold trade and in the building of naval power. However, his persistent and unhurried course indicates that he followed a distant and long-range objective. In the early years the in-

15

stitute at Sagres had his principal attention, sending an occasional expedition south beyond the last point previously known. Beyond Cape Blanco the Portuguese met the first Negroes and brought some back as slaves. By the end of Henry's life exploration and trade had reached only to Sierra Leone, a locality Hanno had attained in a single voyage from Carthage fifteen hundred years earlier. Discovery rather than gain was Henry's major incentive, for he kept reaching deeper into his own pockets and those of his order. He was committing Portugal to the circumnavigation of Africa, and his successors continued on that course.

It is an obligate inference that the scholars at Sagres shared the common learning of cosmography, that they knew the Greek determination of the spherical Earth and checked it by astronomical observation, and also that they accepted the Greek concept of the universal ocean surrounding all lands.[4] By such knowledge and premise a sea route to India was sought, going south around Africa. Alternatively, one might sail west to India across the ocean. The first was the prime objective; the search for a route west was also undertaken.

The Azores Islands (map 2) were discovered by search rather than by chance, according to Diogo Gomes, a navigator knighted in the service of Prince Henry.[5] Gomes said

[4] Angel de Altolaguirre y Duvale, *Cristobal Colón y Pablo del Pozzo Toscanelli* (Madrid, 1908), devoted his second chapter to medieval concepts of the form of the Earth, citing in number scholars who held it to be a sphere. Sacrobosco's thirteenth-century *Treatise of the Sphere* was well known to cosmographers, for example. It may be added that Sacrobosco (John of Holywood) was familiar to cosmographers and navigators in Portugal by the contacts of the time between Portugal and Britain.

[5] Diogo Gomes, participant in the Portuguese discoveries and colonization in the "western ocean sea," gave an account to Martin Behaim (*ca.* 1480). This found its way, by a Latin version, into a large collection of items, texts and maps, which a German printer in Lisbon, known as Valentim Fernandes, assembled on Portuguese seafaring of the fifteenth century. Valentim ended his compilation in 1507 and left it unprinted. By good fortune it found its way to the Library of Munich, where it was accessible to scholars. The Portuguese Academy of History in 1940 published it in full as *O Manuscrito "Valentim Fernandes."* (Maps 3 and 4 are taken from it.)

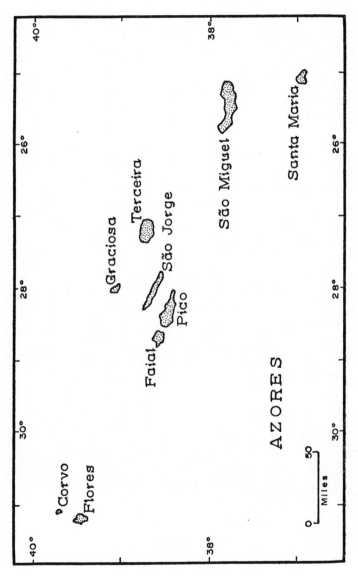

Map 2. Azores Islands.

that "Prince Henry, wishing to have knowledge of farther parts of the western ocean, whether there were islands or mainland beyond the cosmography of Ptolemy, sent caravels at one time to seek land. They sailed and discovered land three hundred leagues to the west of Finisterre." Five of the Azores islands he said were then named, Terceira being so called because it was the third seen. All were uninhabited, for the most part well wooded, and teemed with bird life, especially hawks and falcons, which provided the name Azores. The prince was greatly pleased with the news of this discovery of an attractive group of islands a thousand miles west of Portugal. The Gomes account that the discovery was made by an expedition sent to search for land in the western sea is acceptable (there were earlier sightings, some think). The attention to the bird life suggests that the sailors watched and were guided by the flight of the birds.

The discovery of the Azores has been dated at 1432, based on the Vallsequa map of 1439, which has been read as giving the date of discovery as 1432. Armando Cortesão has studied the original and gives the inscription as "aquestas islas foran trobados p diego de silves pelot del rey de portogall an lay MCCCCXXVIJ," assuring us that the date is clearly legible as 1427.[6] This places their effective discovery at the time when Madeira was being colonized. Madeira needed to be made a going concern as a way station to support the African enterprise.

Meanwhile, so Gomes continued, Prince Henry sent a knight of the Order of Christ back to the Azores, the caravels loaded with pigs, cattle, and fowl. Thus the islands of Santa Maria and São Miguel were stocked with domestic animals, to be left to themselves. A writ of July 1439 told that the prince had placed sheep on all seven Azores islands then known and was ready to begin colonizing them. The

---

[6] A. Cortesão, p. 55.

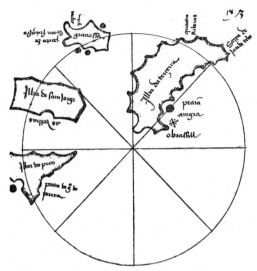

Map 3. Azores According to Valentin Fernandes (before 1507).

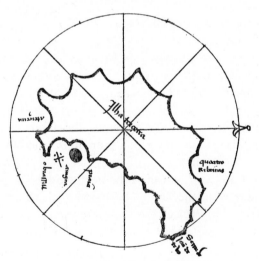

Map 4. Terceira Island (Valentin Fernandes).

hawks, one may infer, took care of the fowl, but the rest of the stock thrived. When colonists were sent they found on all seven islands an abundance of the animals of Portuguese husbandry, providing sustenance while the colony got under way.

Settlement of the Azores began in 1439 or very shortly thereafter, the colonists being on record in 1443 as having been given tax exemptions. The donatory was usually a noble, who brought tenants and workmen. In 1450 a Flemish immigration of importance began. In that year Prince Henry made one Jakobus of Bruges the donatory of part of the island of Terceira, and followed this grant by others to Flemings. Portuguese-Flemish trade relations were strengthened at the time by royal family ties, Henry's sister Isabel (as noted) being the wife of Philip the Good of Burgundy, and Bruges their favorite residence. Ships from Flanders brought settlers and horses in number to the Azores, first to Terceira and then to Faial and Pico, which together became known as the Flemish Islands.[7]

In his unhurried manner Prince Henry made a successful enterprise of the Azores. The donatories carried the costs of development, largely by increase of the livestock that had preceded them. Diogo Gomes reported that the great number of animals in the islands provided a yearly export to Portugal, giving special mention to the large number of swine, and also stating that each year ships sailed there from Portugal to load wheat.

Flores and Corvo, far to the northwest of the main island cluster, were the last to be found and occupied; they were conveyed in Prince Henry's last testament but probably were not settled until after his death in 1460. In the span of

---

[7] E. G. Ravenstein, *Martin Behaim: His Life and His Globe* (London, 1908), pp. 47–50, traced the relations between Portugal and Flanders in the fifteenth century, the prominent Flemish families who came to the Azores, and their intermarriage with Portuguese gentry.

twenty years the archipelago in mid-ocean had become part of rural Portugal, a land of country gentry, farmers, and fishermen with a sizable Flemish enclave destined to be absorbed into a common stock and ways.

The ocean crossing of a thousand miles between the Azores and Portugal and twice that distance from Flanders was passed over by the chroniclers without comment. There is early note of the use of caravels, and little else. The transport of livestock, grain, goods, and persons had become routine. The Azores and even more so the Madeira islands were a canny and profitable investment. The grantees bore the costs, and the Crown shared the profits, modest in the Azores but large from the sugar and wine of Madeira. By midcentury the two island colonies had become mainstays of the Portuguese economy. Each held a key position in the master plan of exploration which Prince Henry was shaping, Madeira as base for the African voyages, the Azores for the western ocean. The great southern objective has diverted historical attention from the alternative western one. Henry organized both the island bases to produce revenues, and from both he had farther exploration in mind.

The Azores were discovered, according to Diogo Gomes, in the search for land beyond the limits of Ptolemaic cosmography. The scholars assembled at Sagres had been engaged in studying the classics and observing the heavens. The shape of the Earth inevitably was central to their discussions, nor were they bound by clerical dogma. Learned men of the time held the Earth to be a globe, and therefore a western crossing of the ocean might be feasible. Such a possibility was probably in the mind of Prince Henry when he settled the Azores and established there a selected lot of noble families.

There were repeated reconnaissances into the western sea during his lifetime. The two outlying islands of Flores and Corvo were thus discovered, perhaps incidental to a wider sweep of the ocean. This particular voyage of discovery has become a widely known part of the background of Columbus, as related by his son Ferdinand. According to it Columbus, living at the monastery of La Rabida adjacent to Palos in Andalusia, met a Spanish pilot who had served under one Diogo de Teive when this Portuguese gentleman set out from Faial in the Azores.[8] They sailed a hundred and fifty leagues into the western sea in search of the Seven Cities of the legend current at the time. They swung so far to the northeast as to sight Cape Clear in Ireland, and on their return chanced to discover Flores. This took place, according to Ferdinand, about forty years before Columbus made his voyage of discovery. (The more probable date is 1457.) It has even been surmised that the party might have gotten to Newfoundland, as noted by Cortesão.

By another document a son of Diogo de Teive was given rights in 1476 to transfer his title to islands called Foreyras, which had been discovered by his father and himself.[9] It is not known what the date of discovery was nor where the islands were supposed to be. Maps of the times showed western islands, some imaginary, some perhaps real.

However much is apocryphal of sailings west of the Azores, there were such, the Azores being the base for search for farther lands and colonized with that intent.

## ALFONSO V, TOSCANELLI, AND THE DANISH EXPEDITION

Alfonso V, called the African, wasted a good deal of the substance of Portugal in trying to conquer Moroccan territory. Discovery down the African coast was supported by a private contract that provided for extension at the rate

[8] A. Cortesão, p. 73, and Hennig, vol. 3, ch. 182.
[9] Hennig, vol. 4, p. 283.

of a hundred leagues a year. The concession ran to 1474—significant date—and was carried out as agreed. The Guinea coast was run out to the head of that gulf, and its southward turn was then followed to the Equator. Africa was taking an unexpected shape, no one knowing how far it might reach into the southern hemisphere. The route to India turned out to be far longer than had been expected.

Alfonso, ruling from 1443 to 1481, had been taught what he knew of maritime matters by his uncle Prince Henry. It was time by 1474, when the African contract expired, to recall what he had been told of alternate possibilities of getting to India. Therefore he addressed himself for advice to the mathematician and cosmographer then of greatest repute, Paolo Toscanelli in Florence, the correspondence being through the king's chaplain as intermediary. Toscanelli replied on June 25, 1474, the year when the contract to explore the African coast ran out. He began by referring to the many previous times he had spoken of another and shorter way to the Indies by crossing the sea instead of by way of Guinea. He continued, the king wished a declaration and demonstration of this better route, with which he complied by sending its description, accompanied by a sea chart drawn by his own hand (since lost). The proper representation would have been by globe, he said, but the chart was less difficult to make or understand. The description of how the ocean should be crossed followed, holding always to the west, with the distances greatly underestimated. (The Asiatic localities were taken from the accounts of Marco Polo, nearly two hundred years old.) In conclusion Toscanelli placed himself at the disposal of the king for further consultation.

Toscanelli supported the idea of sailing west across the ocean, which had already been under consideration by Alfonso and was well known to cosmographers and, as I have suggested, led Prince Henry to discover and colonize the

23

Azores. There was no problem of feasibility other than distance. To remove such objection Toscanelli presented his greatly erroneous calculation of the size of the Earth and also introduced intermediate way stations of Antilia and Cipango (Japan). Of the three versions of the Toscanelli letter, all copies of uncertain origin, the Latin one says "from Antilia known to you," the Italian one "from Antilia, which you call Seven Cities, whereof you have notice," and the Spanish one "the Isle of Antilia which you call Seven Cities, whereof we have notice."

Both legendary islands or island groups were, it seems, accepted in Portugal at the time as factual. Armando Cortesão has traced the first notice of Antilia to a map of 1424. The Seven Cities legend was old and derived from Roderick, last king of the Visigoths, who was overthrown by the Moors about 711. Seven bishops and their people were said to have fled to Portugal, where they took ship to settle on a great island and built seven cities. The historical voyage of Teive from the Azores in the 1450's had the Seven Cities as objective. The badly preserved Weimar (or Freducci) chart of the 1460's has been read by Cortesão as showing an island named *antilia septe civit,* indicating that by then the two legends had merged into one.

Toscanelli had nothing to present that was new, except his reduction of distance, open to challenge by Portuguese cosmographers. No action was taken by Alfonso. Western exploration would continue, provided it was not done at his expense. Some of the gentry of the Azores were prosperous, and occasionally one offered to equip a ship and search the western sea for the Seven Cities or some other new land. Alfonso granted licenses to discover, possess, and govern with or without designation of what was to be found. Some may never have sailed; others did so without result. The licenses were transferable. Thus the Teive license given by Prince

Henry was passed by Alfonso to Diogo Telles in 1476, to "find the Seven Cities or other inhabited islands that at present are not being sailed to."

Alfonso would not or could not commit his own resources to western exploration, another war with Castile being imminent. However, he took advantage of an old friendship with Denmark, urged Christian I to explore to the west, and offered to send along a trusted nobleman, João Vaz Corte Real. The antecedent connections between the two countries go back to the time of Prince Henry. Parts of the story have long been known. It remained for Sophus Larsen, Royal Librarian at Copenhagen, to join them in his *Discovery of North America Twenty Years Before Columbus* (1924). Dom Pedro had been at the court in Copenhagen and brought back geographical data, apparently including a map, to his brother Henry (1428), thus beginning relations between the two courts. Azurara's *Cronica*, completed in 1450, told of a nobleman of the Danish court, named Vallarte (Wollert) who got permission to go to the court of Prince Henry in 1448. The latter provided the Dane with a caravel and sent him to Cape Verde as his emissary, bearing letters to a great lord of Senegal. According to Azurara, the Dane and his landing party were captured by the Negroes, the caravel returning to Portugal. Other Danish adventurers joined Portuguese forces in the Moroccan wars.

Denmark was a major and prosperous power in the north, owning Norway, Iceland, the Faeroes, and nominally Greenland. It had the background, means, and location to take up exploration of the long-neglected northern seas and accepted the proposal made by Alfonso to Christian I.

The four leading participants in the voyage are historically known, the two German sea captains Pining and Pothorst, the Scandinavian pilot latinized as Scolvus, and the Portuguese guest João Vaz Corte Real. Pining later was governor of Iceland, from 1478 to his death in 1490. Both Germans had been in Danish services and perhaps as such were defamed as pirates in English and Hanse quarters. Scolvus was described as an intrepid seafarer by a half-dozen treatises of the sixteenth century, with the notion that he made an independent voyage beyond Greenland. Three of these later accounts assign the date as 1476. On the Gemma Frisius globe (1527?), followed by the globe of L'Ecluy, Scolvus was thus placed as having reached the Arctic northwest (America), where the "Quij people" lived, whoever they were. The Dutch historian Wytfliet had him get to a western land within the Arctic circle. The Spanish historian López de Gómara brought him to Labrador with men from Norway. Perhaps all drew on a single lost source.

João Vaz Corte Real was named governor of Terceira in April 1474, establishing there one of the principal families of the Azores. The sixteenth-century Jesuit Gaspar Fructuoso, native and resident of the Azores, wrote that, at the time of his appointment, João Vaz had returned from the discovery of the land of the Bacalhaos, meaning roughly Newfoundland. The 1474 date of his appointment in the Azores is secure. Cordeyro, a later and more careful historian than Fructuoso, agreed that João Vaz had gone to the Bacalhaos on orders of the king before he was appointed governor. For this reason Larsen placed the voyage in 1472 or 1473.

The thesis of Larsen has stood up well.[10] The Danish voyage, according to Larsen, preceded the Toscanelli letter, the idea of a western passage having already been in Alfonso's mind. That such a Danish expedition was made into the northwest in the early seventies is not questioned. There is neutral testimony that it was undertaken at the instigation of Alfonso, who sent along a participant observer. Some

[10] Hennig, vol. 4, pp. 247–274, has reviewed data and criticism; see also Stefansson, vol. 1, pp. xxxiv–xxxix.

have thought the voyage was directed to Greenland, which does not make sense. Greenland had been known for centuries. Its Norse colony was failing but was then still in existence, and by the evidence of a cemetery (to be noted later) still had contact with Europe. If there were new "lands and islands in the north" to be found, they lay beyond Greenland. For Christian it was a small matter to do as Alfonso wished. There might be something to the old Norse stories of interesting lands beyond Greenland, which would fall under his jurisdiction. He had paid little attention thus far to his western territories, nor did he do anything more after the voyage than to put Pining in charge of Iceland, to revise its laws and administration. The Corte Real family held a leading position in the Azores and years later was to return to the northwestern sea quest.

## JOHN II AND COLUMBUS

The reign of John II (1481–1495) organized the African trade and pushed discovery southward. Bartholomeu Dias returned in 1488 to announce that he had turned Africa's long-sought southern end, to which the King gave the name Cape of Good Hope. The western ocean thus became of little concern to Lisbon. Azorians might still get permits to explore and possess for the asking, provided they defrayed the costs. Such a license was given in 1486 to Fernão Dulmo, a Fleming who was captain on Terceira. He was authorized to discover the Island of the Seven Cities and be their governor, this as usual to be done at his own expense and hazard. In a later order, since Dulmo was unable to furnish a second caravel, a citizen of Madeira was named to share half the costs and benefits. After leaving Terceira Dulmo was ordered to direct the caravels for the first forty days, thereafter the Madeiran, thus showing that a long voyage was anticipated. There is no further record of this voyage, nor of later ones

27

in the time of John II, for the passing of the southern extremity assured the success of the southern route.

Columbus found no place for himself in the Portuguese operations. The dozen years or so that he spent in Portugal are largely a blank except for the tales his son wrote, some of which Angel de Altolaguirre showed to be contrary to the facts. There are few suggestions as to how Columbus made his living, which was obscure and insecure. He had dreamed of great discovery and had read what he could. It is doubtful that he had taught himself cosmography or even cartography. It may well be, as Altolaguirre thought, that knowing Toscanelli's letter Columbus began to organize his great project on the model drawn by Toscanelli. The letter was in possession of the Portuguese court in 1474. We do not know when or how Columbus learned of it. The copy he solicited and got from Toscanelli is of unknown date but must have been sent before 1482, the time of Toscanelli's death. The covering note by the Florentine to Columbus has been attacked as a fraud, but seems genuine. However Columbus learned of the letter, the original was known in Lisbon. In his conclusion, Altolaguirre wrote that he thought to have shown "that Toscanelli was not a great geographer; that the project attributed to him is authentic, and that the Admiral [Columbus] was guided solely and exclusively by it, as well in offering himself to Portugal as to Castile to go to discover oriental lands."[11]

Columbus appears to have been heard with attention and courtesy at the court of King John but failed to impress the experts. He was neither navigator nor cosmographer, both being strongly represented at Lisbon. Toscanelli's proposal had been studied there long before Columbus heard of it. The resident scholars can hardly have failed to object to

[11] Altolaguirre, p. 339.

its reduction of the size of the Earth. And why no mention of the Azores as starting place into the unknown west? The Seven Cities had been the object of Portuguese search and still were, Dulmo being licensed at that time to go from the Azores to seek them. Enough had been learned of the ocean beyond the Azores to know it to be of great extent; Dulmo was to direct the ships from the first forty days and then to pass the command to the other captain. The Portuguese were aware that a western crossing was a far greater undertaking than Toscanelli or Columbus imagined. They had mariners who had sought it and would continue to do so. A stranger, inexperienced as navigator and without funds, coming to ask the Crown to bear all costs and, according to his son, to receive vast benefits and rights in perpetuity was obviously at the wrong place and at the wrong time. When Bartholomeu Dias returned to Lisbon in December 1488 to announce that he had passed the Cape of Good Hope, Columbus decided to try elsewhere.

# CHAPTER III NEWFOUNDLAND AND FARTHER COASTS

## TRANSATLANTIC POSSESSIONS AT THE END OF THE FIFTEENTH CENTURY

Portugal was first to begin overseas discovery and exploitation as a state enterprise. Prince Henry gave new direction to the course of history by planned exploration and founding of ultramarine colonies. In 1479, Portugal conceded possession of the Canary Islands to Castile, which thereby took its initial venture into colonial empire. Columbus staked out a vast claim for Spain in 1492 by three months in the West Indies. England entered tentatively at the end of the century into what shortly was called the "new found land."

The start of dominion overseas was not by conquest except for the Canaries, where the native Guanches made stout resistance. The Madeira and Azores islands were uninhabited and were given by the Portuguese Crown as seignories to be settled with agriculturists. Later, royal licenses were given to discover and possess new islands, peopled or not. By the time Spain and England began explorations, formal procedures of taking title were practiced; Columbus planted the royal standard at his landing in 1492. The map that Juan de la Cosa drew for the Spanish authorities in 1500 thus delineated and acknowledged the overseas claims of Spain, Portugal, and England (map 5). On it the standard of Portugal marked the Azores, Madeira, and Cape

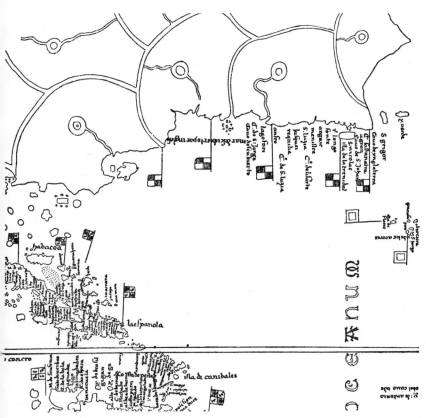

Map 5. Juan de la Cosa Map of 1500 (reproduced from Kretschmer Atlas).

Verde islands; that of Castile the Canaries, the Greater Antilles, and the north coast of Tierra Firme (South America) as far as it had been discovered. Cosa placed English flags along a great western continental coast across from Britain —the first rude, actual showing of North America on a map—acknowledging that the English Crown held title to those parts.

31

# NORTHERN MISTS

Except for the voyage of John Cabot, English and Portuguese discoveries in Canadian waters owed little to Columbus. English ships had crossed the Atlantic before Columbus. The sons of João Vaz Corte Real took up the search for a western passage, following the course their father had taken on the Danish voyage a generation earlier. The "discovery" of the northwestern American coasts came about mainly because the English and Portuguese had common knowledge and parallel interests.

Late studies have placed these northern discoveries in new light. Professor D. B. Quinn proposed his *Argument for the English Discovery of America Between 1480 and 1494* in the *Geographical Journal* of September 1961. In 1962 James A. Williamson published *The Cabot Voyages and Bristol Discovery* as Volume CXX of the Hakluyt Society. Both made intensive use of a lately discovered document known as the John Day letter, first seen by Professor H. Keniston, misfiled under Brazil in the Archive of Simancas in Spain. Keniston called it to the attention of Dr. L. H. Vigneras, who published it in 1956.[1] The letter was written in the winter of 1497–98 and fills major gaps in our knowledge.

## THE JOHN DAY LETTER

John Day was an English merchant engaged in business in Spain, where he had connections with the Spanish Lord Grand Admiral. The latter had asked him to collect information as to what the English knew and were doing in the western sea, in other words to act as intelligence agent for the Spanish Admiralty. The letter, written in Spanish, was in answer to several requests. In addition to the voyagings of John Cabot, it told of prior English discoveries of the west.

---

[1] L. H. Vigneras, *Hispanic-American Historical Review*, vol. 36, pp. 503–509.

# NEWFOUNDLAND AND FARTHER COASTS

My literal translation is shortened only as to epistolary flourishes.

It is of interest that the Spanish Admiralty was keeping watch on events at sea, including high latitudes. The Lord Grand Admiral was identified correctly by Vigneras as Don Fadrique Hernández, Marqués of Tarifa, senior grandee of Castile. Several English commentators have mistaken the admiral for Columbus. Columbus was not the head of the Admiralty, nor was he connected with it. He did not rate address in the terms of respect used in the letter. His presence in Spain at that time was to solicit help for Española, which was in sorry straits, and for no other purpose. The honorific title of admiral he had exacted as part of his contract did not admit him to the counsels of state. He was in fact, shortly to lose the governorship of the Indies he had found.

The John Day letter reads:

> The servant of Your Lordship has brought your letter. Having noted what is requested therein, I am most happy to oblige. The book *Inventio Fortunata* I cannot find, although I thought that I had brought it with my things and am sorry not to find it.[2] The other one by Marco Polo and a copy of the land that has been discovered I am sending. [The next sentence is unclear and unimportant.] I made this in a hurry before my departure. Your Lordship will be apprised of what you wish to know from the said copy. On this copy the capes and islands of the mainland are named, and on it you will also see where the first sight of land was had. The greater part of the land was discovered after they turned back [east]. And also Your Lordship will see that the cape nearest to Ireland lies 1,800 miles west of Dursey Head, which is in Ireland, and the lower end of the Island of the Seven Cities lies to the west of the river of Bordeaux.
>
> Also Your Lordship will know that he [John Cabot] landed at only one place on the mainland, near where they first sighted land. At this place they landed and raised a cross and the banners bearing the coat of arms of the Holy Father and of the King of England, my master. They found large trees of which masts of ships are made and other trees beneath these and a land of much herbage. Here, as I have told Your Lordship, they came

[2] This is a lost fourteenth-century treatise on polar and subpolar regions, written by a friar of Oxford.

33

upon a very narrow lane that led inland and saw a place where a fire had been made, and found dung of beasts [*alimanias*] which they thought were of the field [*campinas*], and they found a stick a cubit long, pierced at each end and carved, which stick was painted red [*con brasil*], and by these tokens it is thought to be an inhabited country. Since he happened to have but a few men, he dared not enter inland farther than a crossbow shot, took on fresh water, and returned to his ship.

Proceeding along the coast they found many fish such as in Iceland customarily are dried in the air and are sold to England and other parts, and these fish are called stockfish [*estoqfis*] in England; and coasting along they also saw two figures on land, one running behind the other, not knowing whether they were persons or animals. It appeared to them that they saw cultivated fields where they thought people lived. They saw woodland [*floresta*] with beautiful leaves.

It was the end of May when he left England and he was under way for thirty-five days before finding land, the wind being east and northeast, and the sea quiet both going and returning, except for one day of storm, which was two or three days before coming to the land. Going so far out, the needle of the compass failed to point north and fell off two points. They went on for about a month discovering the coast, and from the above-mentioned cape of the mainland that is nearest to Ireland they returned to the coast of Europe in fifteen days with a following wind, landing in Brittany because the seamen distracted him by saying that he was headed too far to the north. From there he came to Bristol and went to see the King in order to relate all that was told above, and the King gave him a grant of twenty pounds a year for his support. As time goes on more will become known of this matter, for it is hoped, God willing, to employ ten or twelve of the ships in the coming year for further discovery of the said land. In the present year he went with but a single ship of fifty tons and twenty men and with supplies for seven or eight months, for which reason this [repeated] effort is to be undertaken.

It is held to be certain that the cape of the said land was found and discovered in other times [*en otros tiempos*] by those of Bristol who discovered Brasil and is presumed and believed to be the mainland that the men of Bristol found.

As to the first voyage [of John Cabot] about which Your Lordship wishes to know, it was made in one ship, and the crew he took thwarted him, and he was poorly provisioned and found the weather contrary and so elected to turn back. . . .

The letter informed the Spanish Admiralty on a number of matters concerning the northern ocean and higher latitudes: (1) It gives the fullest and geographically clearest account of the John Cabot discovery. (2) It mentions an unsuccessful prior attempt by Cabot which was already known to the Lord Admiral. (It is not recorded in histories.) (3) It identifies the land Cabot found with an earlier discovery (*en otros tiempos*) by men of Bristol. (4) This earlier discovery had been called Brasil by the Bristol discoverers, and was believed to be mainland. (This Brasil was an Irish name for a legendary island to the west, as will be noted later.) (5) This pre-Cabot discovery had also been known to his lordship. (6) Day made a hasty copy of a map of the discovered land. (This is the likely source of that part of the Juan de la Cosa map of 1500.) (7) That Day was asked to get a copy of Marco Polo suggests that it was not available in Spain. It also supports the inference of Altolaguirre that Columbus knew Marco Polo's geography of the Far East at second hand through the letter of Toscanelli.

The John Day letter adds a good deal to and confirms what had been known of English ventures across the western sea, and it establishes English discovery of the American continent prior to Columbus. It also tells that the Spanish Admiralty was keeping abreast of maritime activities elsewhere.

## FROM BRISTOL TO THE HIGH SEA

Bristol, at the time England's first port facing the open Atlantic, flourished throughout the fifteenth century by ventures out on the high seas. Early in the century it entered the Iceland trade. Herring were the main product loaded in Iceland. Bristol customs records also listed *stokffish* (dried cod) and *titeling* (dried ling) as cargoes from Iceland.[3] Bristol developed the import of wines from the south of France while this region was still in English hands. When Madeira became a supplier of sugar and wine, Bristol

---

[3] Williamson, Docs. 1 and 5.

merchants were the purveyors to northern markets. No other waterfront of the time knew as much of the northern Atlantic.

Perhaps because Bristol had a privileged position with regard to Ireland, the ancient Irish legend of the Isle of Brasil took root there. Its quest from Bristol has been documented as far back as 1480.[4] On July 15, 1480 John Lloyd, "the most knowledgeable seaman of the whole of England," sailed from Bristol "for the Island of Brasylle." He was reported as returning to an Irish port on September 18, having been driven back by storm without finding the island. On July 6, 1481 two balingers (cargo ships) cleared from Bristol for the purpose of "examining and finding a certain island called the Isle of Brasil." The ships belonged to a partnership of Bristol merchants. It is known by Bristol records that the ships sailed and returned but not what they found. The chief participant, one Thomas Croft, was given exemption of duty on forty bushels of salt loaded on each ship as not being merchandise but for "the intent to search and fynde the Isle of Brasile." This might satisfy the customs record, but why so much salt unless it was to be used as Professor Quinn has surmised, for salting fish at a western fishing ground already known to Bristol? If men of Bristol had discovered the great fishery off Newfoundland, they might not have advertised it in a public record.

Were these then "the other times" which Day mentioned, when Bristol men discovered the Isle of Brasil that probably was a mainland? Day was confirming knowledge that had reached the Admiral of Castile earlier.

There is further documentary support of early voyages from Bristol across the Atlantic. Pedro de Ayala had been sent to London as intelligence agent of the Spanish Crown. A letter by him in cipher, written July 1498, said: "For the

[4] D. B. Quinn, pp. 277–285; Williamson, ch. 2 and Docs. 6 and 7.

past seven years the people of Bristol have equipped two, three, or four caravels to go in search of the island of Brasil and the Seven Cities, according to the fancy of this Genoese,"[5] the Genoese being John Cabot. Cabot is thought to have come to England in 1495, so that his fantasia cannot have prompted the Bristol voyages. Perhaps Cabot attached the name of the island of Seven Cities to that of Brasil, used in Bristol. The legend of the Seven Cities had long been current in Portugal and Spain; perhaps he thought it gave added attraction to his plans. Ayala informed his sovereigns that for seven years past Bristol had been sending two or more ships to go in search of Brasil, which would place the beginnings of the search in 1491 or earlier. Day's statement that men of Bristol had found the western land years earlier, "in other times," would hardly have been used for voyages between 1491 and 1497, the years immediately preceding the time Day wrote. Bristol merchants were finding it profitable to continue to send ships west across the sea; they did so before Cabot came to England, and before the discovery of Columbus. Was the name Brasil a convenient cover for their extension of cod fisheries from Bristol to American shores? By the quantity of salt taken west from Bristol in 1481, the conjecture is that the congregation of cod along the American shores was known then and that they were being taken there.

## THE VOYAGES OF JOHN CABOT

The role of John Cabot has been revised and reduced by the studies of Williamson and Quinn. The admirable Williamson monograph serves as basis for the following section. Williamson has shown that Cabot was almost certainly born in Genoa and secured Venetian citizenship around 1472, a condition of which was that he had been

[5] H. P. Biggar, *Precursors of Cartier* (1911), pp. 27–29.

domiciled in Venice for at least fifteen years. It would seem that Cabot was well in his fifties when he got to England, probably in 1495. In Venice he had been a merchant's factor; it was said that he had been to Mecca "whither spices are borne by caravan" (Soncino, infra). The Spanish historian Ballesteros-Gabrois has identified a Venetian John Cabot in Valencia from 1490 to the spring of 1493, promoting plans for harbor works that came to nothing. If this is our Cabot he would have been in Spain when Columbus returned from his voyage of discovery. There is very little known about Cabot until late in his middle age when he came to England with his wife and sons, apparently in 1495. Soncino, ambassador in London of the Duke of Milan, reported in 1497 that Cabot had come to England a poor man but won support of Bristol merchants which gave him credence at court. Having made his voyage of discovery he was going about London being called Admiral and promising noble estates to his friends and bishoprics to poor Italian friars. Soncino added that he might well have had an archbishopric but had "reflected that the benefices which your Excellency reserves for me are safer."[6]

Cabot, Soncino wrote, "has the description of the world in a map, and also in a solid sphere, which he has made. . . . Having observed that the sovereigns of Portugal and of Spain had occupied unknown islands, he decided to make a similar acquisition for his Majesty." Having found land across the sea he "has his mind set upon even greater things, because he proposes to keep along the coast from the place at which he touched, more and more towards the east [Far East] until he reaches an island which he calls Cipango, situated in the equinoctial regions, where he believes that all the spices of the world have their origin, as well as the jewels." In other words, he would take ship west across the sea to the land that

[6] Williamson, Doc. 24.

had been visited from Bristol and thence go on southwestward into the equinoctial regions of the Asiatic spice lands. Columbus obviously had not found them and was not looking farther than the islands he had discovered. Thus Cabot looked to England as sponsor, proposing a direct western crossing and then a southwest course that would take him into tropical waters. That he went straight to Bristol to present his plan indicates that he knew of the Bristol discovery, as Quinn has suggested. Having verified the crossing from Bristol to America he was ready for the grand voyage. Soncino continued: "He tells all this in such a way, and makes everything so plain, that I also feel compelled to believe him."

Cabot went ahead rapidly with his project, receiving his first letters patent from the King on March 5, 1496. Since the discovery of the John Day letter it is known that Cabot made a first unsuccessful attempt out of Bristol in 1496. The following May, in 1497, he was off again from Bristol in a bark of eighteen or twenty men. Bristol supplied the ship, sailors, and funds as a modest venture, the King only the license. The voyage took less than three months, Williamson giving preference to the time from May 20 to August 6. Land was sighted after five weeks, the coast was followed for about a month, and the return to sight of European shores was made in fifteen days. The men of Bristol were competent sailors, and they had good weather. A single overseas landing was made, at the place of first landfall (June 24?), after which they turned east and north, from time to time in near sight of land.

Where the lone landing was made and how far they coasted thereafter has been the subject of much discussion, reviewed by Williamson. The contemporary data are in three Italian letters and in the Day letter.[7] The first letter from Lorenzo Pasqualigo in London, August 23, 1497, has the

---

[7] Williamson, Docs. 22, 23, 24.

information: "That Venetian of ours who went with a small ship from Bristol to find new islands has come back and says he has discovered mainland 700 leagues away, which is the country of the Grand Khan, and that he coasted it for 300 leagues and landed and did not see any person; but he has brought back to the king certain snares which were spread to take game and a needle for making nets, and he found certain notched trees so that by this he judges that there are inhabitants." A second letter, of August 24, reports that Cabot "has found two very large and fertile new islands. He has also discovered the Seven Cities, 400 leagues from England, on the western passage." The third letter, by Soncino, tells the duke of Milan how the king of England "has gained a part of Asia, without a stroke of the sword." Cabot's companions from Bristol backed him as to the truth of the statements. "They say that the land is excellent and temperate, and they believe that Brazil wood and silk are native there. They assert that the sea there is swarming with fish, which can be taken not only with the net, but in baskets let down with a stone, so that it sinks in the water."

The fourth document is the letter of John Day, previously cited. Day gave the latitudes coasted as being from that of the Gironde estuary to Irish Cape Dursey (45 1/2 to 51 1/2 N. Lat.), which would have been from Cape Breton Island to northern Newfoundland.

The latitudes given are too high. A small bark on a northern sea had poor horizon for celestial observation. The landing (St. John's Day, June 24) was near the westernmost point reached, from which they turned back for about a month, repeatedly in sight of land until they left the cape that was thought to lie west of Ireland. Had the latter position been correct they would have turned north at Cape Race and then northwest along the eastern shore of Newfoundland, an unlikely direction for a ship on its return to

England and one which would have brought them to bleak coasts and icy waters. The month was July, the time of greatest fogs off eastern Newfoundland, with southward-drifting icebergs, and the shore most often hidden by fogbanks. There is no mention of anything of the kind.

At the place where they landed there were tall trees suitable for masts, other trees, and much herbage. From shipboard they saw subsequently an open country that might have been cultivated ground and also attractive and flowering woodland (*floresta*). These descriptions would not apply to Newfoundland, but would be possible for Nova Scotia and proper for New England, where they would have seen tall, well-grown white pines, deciduous hardwoods, and open tracts suitable for grazing and cultivation. In those parts, inhabited by Algonquian Indians, they might indeed have had a distant glimpse of fields. The month they spent coasting northeast (heard by Pasqualigo as covering three hundred leagues) would have taken them in leisurely fashion from New England to Cape Race, whence a favorable passage took them in fifteen days to Europe.

After the preliminary trip of 1497 Cabot set out on the grand voyage to the Orient in 1498, probably in May. Ayala, writing the Spanish sovereigns on July 25, reported that five ships had sailed, provisioned for a year, and that one, badly damaged in a great storm, had returned to an Irish port. The London Chronicles added that the king had provided one ship, stocked with merchandise of London merchants, and that merchants of Bristol had sent three or four more with trade goods.[8] This is the last certain knowledge of Cabot and of that project.

Cabot came to England not as a master navigator but as an applied geographer who would show by the terrestrial globe he carried that England might have its own route to

8 Williamson, Doc. 31.

the Orient. The concept, long familiar to cosmographers and an alternative route of Portuguese exploration, had lately found partial verification by Columbus. Cabot would promote another approach from a northern country which had the ships, mariners, and location for such enterprise. Bristol had mariners who knew the way to a land they called Brasil, across the sea to the west. Cabot would persuade Bristol merchants that by way of that extremity of Asia (so called in the letters of Pasqualigo and Soncino) he would take their trading ships southwest to the Oriental treasure lands. He would persuade the king of England to emulate Portugal and Spain in taking title to overseas domain.

In Cabot's voyage of 1497 formal possession was taken for England of an unknown locality (which may have been in New England or in Nova Scotia). The month-long coasting that followed confirmed the attainment of a mainland, inferred as Asiatic. The news was promptly communicated to Italy and Spain, the John Day letter being an elaboration of earlier word.

The Spanish Crown found itself confronted in 1498 by two overseas dilemmas, the failure of the administration of Columbus and the advance of the English at the north. The state of its Indies had been going from bad to worse under Columbus. Española was in a crisis. The third voyage of Columbus (1498), which was a somewhat dispirited attempt to save the enterprise, discovered the existence of mainland to the south (the Venezuelan Gulf of Paria) a year after Cabot had done so in the north. A greater expedition by Cabot was by then under way to open English trade with the Orient and establish English title along the way. It was time for the Spanish Crown to take countermeasures, first to limit the territory over which Columbus had authority and then to remove him from his position as governor. Alonso de Hojeda, a defected lieutenant of Columbus, was made governor in 1499 of the western part of Tierra Firme, as the mainland coast of the Caribbean was called. He was then given orders to proceed west along that coast in order to block the advance of the English out of the north. The intention of Cabot was known, the loss of his party not as yet. Thereby, except for Labrador and a strait beyond it, ended English engagement in western exploration until the latter sixteenth century, and Spanish advance was left free to west and north.[9]

## THE LABRADOR QUESTION

The name Labrador, it is agreed, derives from a Portuguese, João Fernandes, with the byname *el lavrador*. Such a common name as Fernandes called for an identifying nickname. That he was called "the farmer" carried no implication of social status; King Dinis had been thus known. Until he migrated to England in 1500, the said Fernandes was a landowner and cultivator of means in the Azores island of Terceira, not a small farmer as has been said.

The version supported by Portuguese scholars and based on documents in the Azores and at Lisbon is that Fernandes, in company with one Barcelos, was absent from the Azores for three years (1492–95), exploring by license of King John. Also by license of King Manuel (October 1499) he was again given authority to discover. The second license was too late to be put into effect before his removal to England for reasons unstated. The first voyage has been sharply challenged by Samuel E. Morison in his *Portuguese Voyages to America in the Fifteenth Century* (summary in

[9] The Cosa map presented a continual land body west of the Ocean Sea from the Arctic to well below the equator, the northern coast trending southwestward beyond Cuba, masked by the framed figure of St. Christopher. By this device Cosa avoided committing himself as to whether the northern land was joined to the Tierra Firme of the south, as was suggested by the orders to Hojeda and shortly was proved.

Williamson). As the evidence stands, the 1492 Fernandes exploration is unproven and the 1499 license not used. It is of interest that the Azores continued to be the Portuguese outpost from which men offered to go at their own expense to explore the far sea. That the direction was to the northwest is inferred from the part Fernandes took shortly thereafter in England.

The next item of record are letters patent of March 1501 by King Henry VII to three named merchants of Bristol and three named "Esquires of the islands of the Azores," residing at Bristol, one being John Fernandes. Permission was given to sail any seas including the Arctic, before or then unknown to Christians. The grant therefore excluded parts previously visited from Bristol and indicated that their course would be to the north thereof, in other words to the land since known as Labrador. There are several documentary notations that two voyages were made under this patent; one reported bringing hawks (falcons?), and one three savages taken in the new found land. Additional and more inclusive letters patent were issued on December 9, 1502, including the two Azorians previously named but not John Fernandes, who seems to disappear from further notice. This may have been the preliminary to what was known by 1506 as the Company of Adventurers to the New Found Lands, a term that was coming into use for whatever English activities were going on across the sea from Bristol. Thus far I have followed the exposition of Williamson.

This leaves unanswered the question of the origin of Labrador as a geographic term, which still is unclear. It begins to appear on maps about 1502, first in Italy, where most maps were made and where the latest information was most quickly entered. News of new lands was placed on maps in haste, the mapmakers knowing nothing of their location, size, or form. Usually the entries were shown as islands. One cartographer copied another or relied on his imagination and decorative sense. On such early Italian maps and their derivatives, a land called Labrador was shown conspicuously in the northwestern or northern part of the ocean, sometimes as a wedge having some resemblance to the shape of Greenland. I am unable to follow Williamson and Skelton, who say that João Fernandes sailed to Greenland "beyond reasonable doubt,"[10] and instead incline to the opinion of Sofus Larsen that such "identification of Greenland with Labrador is a capricious fancy of ignorant Italian map makers."[11] This northern sea would wait years before charts were made with knowledge of distance and direction. A landing in Greenland could hardly have missed the Norse settlement or its ruins, conspicuously situated at Herjolfsness, the southern approach to the land. Why a new name or a direction bearing to the known north?

The bits of information carry linked clues. João Fernandes was given a patent by the Portuguese king to discover and govern and shortly thereafter left his Azores home to settle in Bristol. The first guess is that he had a sharp disappointment at home, such as that a similar license had been given to Gaspar Corte Real, of whom more below. The other is that he was given inducement to come to Bristol because of knowledge he had. Ships had been going west across the sea from Bristol for twenty years, had experience of the wealth of fish on the other side of the sea, and had made reconnaissance of western coasts under Cabot. Arrived at Bristol, Fernandes was brought into a consortium of Bristol merchants with two other Azorians established at Bristol. The March 1501 date of issue of the lengthy and carefully drawn up letters patent shows that no time was lost in preparing the new enterprise. The terms of the patent declared

[10] Skelton in Williamson, p. 310.
[11] Hennig, vol. 4, p. 267.

the purpose was discovery and possession by England of hitherto unknown lands. The initiative clearly came from merchants of Bristol who had been in contact with the Azores and had a new exploration in mind. This may have been, as Williamson has surmised, the finding of a western passage in high latitudes. It has been suggested that such an idea had been in the minds of Portuguese from the time of Prince Henry, the Azores being the outpost from which to look in that direction. When merchants of Bristol became interested, they sought participation from Azorian experience.

Such was the credible tradition as it became established and was recorded on maps.[12] For example, a Spanish map of about 1525 (known as Wolfenbüttel B) carries the legend "Land of the Labrador which was discovered by the English of the town of Bristol and because the one who gave the notice (*aviso*) thereof was a labrador of the islands of the Azores it retained this name." Men of Bristol thus may have found Labrador in 1501 by direction of Fernandes el Labrador. It is not known whether he went on the expedition, nor how and when he gained the knowledge that sent the ships on their course of discovery. Had he earlier been on a private three years' northwestern exploration out of Terceira (1492–95), as Portuguese students think?

## THE BROTHERS CORTE REAL

The last and most serious Portuguese attempt in the northwest was by Gaspar and Miguel Corte Real, sons of João Vaz who had been captain on Terceira since his return from the Danish expedition. The family had flourished, Gaspar being a gentleman of the king's household and close to King Manuel, as Damião de Góes explained in his *Cronica de D. Manuel*. The royal license of May 12, 1500 to Gaspar

---

[12] Skelton in Williamson, pp. 310–311.

is unusually broad and cordial and begins by acknowledging his past ventures at sea: "In the past you have endeavored by yourself and at your expenses, with ships and men, to seek, discover, and find by much effort and expenditure of your means and in danger of your own person certain islands and mainland and now wish so to continue." Nothing otherwise is known of such earlier efforts.

According to Góes, Gaspar took off into the northwestern sea in the spring of 1500 and returned to Lisbon in autumn. Góes, writing at midcentury, confused this voyage with the one of the following year. A 1500 voyage is known to have taken place but, having begun early in the season, ran into ice floes at the north, sighted some high ground but apparently did not land, and turned back. It is thought to have gotten into ice off the east coast of Greenland and to have sighted its mountain rim.[13]

In May 1501 Gaspar started northwest again, accompanied by Miguel, this time with three ships. A long stretch of the North American coast was explored, largely I think of Newfoundland, as discussed below. Gaspar sent two ships back to Lisbon while he continued the exploration. (Biggar thought that the separation took place in Placentia Bay on the south coast of Newfoundland.) Gaspar and his ship failed to return. Miguel started from Portugal in search of his brother in May 1502, the three ships dispersing for the search with a place of rendezvous arranged. Two met there; the third, Miguel's, did not appear again. It is thought that Miguel followed Gaspar into the Gulf of St. Lawrence. A third brother wished to take up the search in 1503 but was kept at home by King Manuel, who sent two armed vessels without result.

Thus ended the interest of Portugal in the northwestern

[13] The documents were collected by the Canadian Archivist H. P. Biggar in *The Precursors of Cartier* (Ottawa, 1911).

Atlantic. It had been kept alive by the Corte Real family and may be attributed to what the father had learned on the Danish expedition. That the sons exerted themselves so greatly in that direction gives support to the reality of that earlier voyage, still questioned by some. There was no longer any need for Portugal to be concerned with a western passage. India had been reached around Africa before Gaspar set out on his last voyage, and Pedro Cabral, en route to India, had discovered in 1500 the land of Santa Cruz that soon would be renamed Brazil. Portugal was committed to exploiting three continents and could not extend itself in still another direction.

As there had been no formal Portuguese claim to land in the northwest, there was no renunciation. Manuel felt free, as his predecessors had, to grant rights of discovery overseas. Before Portugal and Spain agreed in 1494 on the demarcation of Tordesillas it was finders keepers. After that no one knew where the line, a hundred leagues west of the farthest Azores island would be crossed. Manuel might claim that the land found by the brothers Corte Real lay on his side of the line, or he might claim prior rights going back beyond the treaty, or he might disregard the treaty's application to those parts, as did the king of England. The Cantino map in 1502 entered a large body of land in the northwest as *Terra del Rey de Portuguall*. Other maps of Portuguese origin or bias declared a land or island of Corte Real or of Bacalhaos, the Portuguese name for dried cod. By 1541, when Alonso de Santa Cruz composed his *Islario* for the Spanish Crown, Labrador was named as the farther north of the American mainland and Bacalaos as adjoining it to the south, some features of the latter resembling Nova Scotia and southern Newfoundland. (News of Cartier's explorations [1534, 1535–36] of the Gulf of St. Lawrence had not gotten through to Sevilla.)

Biggar thought that he could trace a Corte Real coasting of Newfoundland by Portuguese names found on sixteenth-century maps, some of which survive to the present, such as Cape Bonavista, Conception Bay, Ferryland (Faralhao), Fermeuse (Fermoso), and Cape Race (Cabo Razo). Newfoundland, Bacalaos, and land of Corte Real were indeterminate and largely equivalent geographical terms.

An orientation of sorts may be found in accounts of the 1501 Corte Real voyage, given in Italian letters, two by Pietro Pasqualigo, one to the seignory of Venice and one to his brother, and a letter from Alberto Cantino to the duke of Ferrara. These were written from Lisbon after the writers visited the returned ships.[14] Damião de Góes secured some additional information.

Pasqualigo, Venetian ambassador in Lisbon, gave his information in terms perhaps inferring a New World. The voyage, he wrote, had gone two thousand miles to unknown land to the northwest (of Lisbon). The caravels were not able to get to the land found the year before (the preliminary voyage) because the sea was frozen. They were able to examine the coast for at least six hundred miles without coming to its end. For this reason and because of the many large rivers they judged it to be mainland. Also it was thought to be connected with the lands belonging to Spain and with "the parrot lands newly discovered by ships of this kingdom [Portugal] on their way to Calicut." (This was the discovery of Brazil by Cabral in 1500). The Portuguese king was pleased to hear that he could get timber in great quantity and in short time for use as masts and spars. Also there was great abundance of salmon, herring, and cod.

By the Cantino account the ships sailed north for four months (the time is exaggerated) and found a sea packed

[14] Biggar, Docs. 7 and 8; Williamson, Doc. 38.

with snow, and farther on with ice, and then turned west to pass along a coast of great rivers, with numerous kinds of fruits (berries of midsummer?) and pine trees that grew to greater size than would serve for masts. Biggar's inference is that capes Bonavista and Race were named on this voyage. From Newfoundland the coastal scrutiny would have continued west and south along Nova Scotia, by the notice of great pines, that both Italians gave. Without knowing that he was doing so, Gaspar Corte Real would thus have been retracing four years later and in the opposite direction the coasting of John Cabot of 1497. The most important note on the country was of the great pine trees, the straight tall white pines of the New World, memorable to men from Portugal.

There were reports on the natives and, more important, natives were brought to Lisbon. Pasqualigo went to see the first of the returned ships and noted:

> They say this country is very populous and the houses of its inhabitants are of long strips of wood covered with the skins of fish. They have brought back seven natives, men, women, and children, and in the other caravel which is expected from hour to hour, fifty others are coming. They resemble gypsies in color, aspect, figure, and stature. They are clothed in the skins of various animals, mainly of otters. In summer they turn the hair outside and in winter the other way. These skins are not sewn together in any manner nor tanned, but are worn just as they are taken from the animals; they wear them over their shoulders and arms. Their private parts are held by cords made of very strong sinews of fish, making them look like wild men. They are very shy and gentle, but excellently formed as to arms and legs and shoulders, beyond describing.

Some of the country the Portuguese saw was said to be populous, the king being pleased at the prospect of many slaves. (They may have found houses of long strips of wood or bark, but these were not covered with skins of fish.)

Cantino went to visit the second caravel which brought fifty men and women. These he had seen and touched. The natives were somewhat taller than average Italians and were well proportioned. The men wore their hair long, like Italians, and put it up in a kind of twist (*anhelate volveture*). Their faces were marked by large designs, like those of Indians (a reference to the natives Cabral had met on the coast of Brazil?). They lived by fishing and hunting (according to Cantino employing bow and arrow) and made use of the skin of a very large and long-haired deer [moose] for their garments, houses, and boats. They had eyes of a greenish cast that gave them a fierce look. Their speech, which was not understood, lacked rough tones and had an agreeable sound. Mien and gesture were most gentle, and they laughed and showed their pleasure freely. So much for the men, Cantino said, and next to take note of the women:

> They have small breasts and most beautiful bodies and are of gentle countenance. Their color may be described as white rather than otherwise, the men being much darker. In sum, except for the guarded looks of the men, they are similar in every other way to ourselves as to features and appearance. They go quite naked except for a skin of the above mentioned deer about their private parts. They have no arms nor any iron, but whatever they fashion and make they do by using very hard and sharp stone, with which they can work anything however hard.

Damião de Góes later added additional information:

> The people are very barbarous and rude, in manner almost like those of the land of Santa Cruz [Brazil, the use of the obsolete name suggesting that he was copying an old source], except that they appear white but are so tanned by cold that the whiteness disappears with age and is dulled. They are of middle stature, very agile, and great bowmen. They use fire-pointed shafts (*paos tostados*) instead of assegais and with as good effect as though they were tipped with fine steel. They clothe themselves in the skins of wild animals in which that land abounds. They live in caverns in the rocks and in huts (*choupanes*). They have no law, believe greatly in auguries, observe marriage, and are very jealous of their wives, in which respect they are like the Lapps.

This was the second Portuguese contact with American natives, the year after Cabral had landed in Brazil. Racially

51

these northern natives gave the impression of being like gypsies, the males like weatherbeaten Europeans, the women of fairer skin. They were not yet recognized as Indians, as those of Brazil were. In Nova Scotia the visitors were in Algonquian, specifically Micmac, territory, and in Newfoundland among Beothuks. The appreciative descriptions of their physique and features would apply to Algonquian tribes, who have provided us with the image of the handsome savage, as in the *Leatherstocking Tales* and *Hiawatha*. The Beothuks are among the least known natives of the New World and were among the earliest in the north to become extinct. It has been determined that they spoke a language not known to be related to any other and that their culture was primitive and unaggressive. Can those early Portuguese and Italian observations be applied to one or the other native people?

The people described were not Eskimos. There is almost nothing that points to Algonquian identification, no mention of birchbark canoes, of buckskin garments or moccasins such as the captives should have worn, of crops or fields, of tomahawks, of any Algonquian traits that should have caught attention. Most significantly there is no word of conflict. Europeans might have visited amicably with Algonquian Indians, but they could not have loaded a ship with captive men, women, and children without hard fighting. Nor would these captives have been gentle, friendly, and laughing. They are not in character for proud and brave Algonquians.

Beothuks did make varied use of the hides of moose, a main game animal of Newfoundland woods and marshes. Unlike the Algonquians, who lived in Quonset-like houses, they lived in small huts and rock shelters. It is not known that they had chiefs or were organized for warfare. It is likely that the loading of a lot of captives would be deferred to the last, when Gaspar sent the two caravels home while he continued exploration. Biggar proposed that this separation took place in Placentia Bay of southern Newfoundland. This would have been a proper place to secure a cargo of guileless Beothuks, who seem to have enjoyed themselves when unloaded in Lisbon, the first and probably only lot of slaves King Manuel got from those parts.[15]

## THE PATTERN OF CHANGE IN THE FIFTEENTH CENTURY

The fifteenth century was the time when medieval Europe turned outward to know and possess the Ocean Sea. It has been said that the restlessness that had found release in the crusades found new outlet and new horizons at sea. Europeans became curious about far and unknown lands, the adventures they might find there, and especially about the wealth they might gain. The age of overseas exploration and exploitation had begun and reached from India to Newfoundland and Labrador. Atlantic ports from Lisbon and Sevilla to Bristol and London had become gateways to the overseas world.

This was the century of Portugal, which rose to first place among seafaring nations and became the first world power. Prince Henry is the great exemplar of the age, who more than anyone else set its course to overseas discovery, commerce, and colonization. Portugal's great new empire was built about the South Atlantic and Indian oceans. We may not overlook Prince Henry's part in pioneering discovery in the North Atlantic. He sent out the ships that discovered the Azores Islands. He organized their colonization and used them to probe farther into the western sea. That he had the Azores in mind as a northern base from which to

---

[15] Diamond Jenness, *Canad. Nat. Mus.*, no. 86, thought that the Corte Real expedition brought Beothuks.

cross the ocean to the Far East is a likely conjecture. The Greek knowledge of the spherical Earth was familiar to the scholars whom he assembled at Sagres and their astronomical observations were thus concerned. The care with which he prepared the settlement of the Azores indicates the expectation of their utility for farther exploration. What his nephew King Alfonso knew of cosmography had come from Prince Henry. The king's inquiry of Toscanelli as to the feasibility of sailing west to gain the Far East tells that he had been thus instructed. This also is the likely explanation of the Danish voyage he besought at the same time. The ill-fated voyages of the brothers Corte Real to Newfoundland, the final Portuguese venture in that direction, were, we may infer, in search of a western passage.

The English were first to cross the western sea, as the record stands. This was by private initiative of seamen and merchants of Bristol, experienced in trade with Iceland, Madeira, and the Azores. Their commerce in fish from Canadian shores may have attracted the Italian Cabot to Bristol. A persuasive promoter, he secured ships and men at Bristol and license to discover and possess from Henry VII. Establishing title by a single brief landing he has minor credit for starting England on her eventual course of empire. Again it was from Bristol and with Bristol capital and participation that an Azorian who had emigrated to Bristol affixed the name Labrador to the northern mainland. An Azorian "squire" and an Italian adventurer have taken the place in history that belongs in larger measure to citizens of Bristol.

Spain, more properly Castile, was last to enter on overseas dominion, by the return of Columbus in the spring of 1493 with news of his discovery. The early enthusiasm soon faded. By the century's end the survival of Española was in doubt, and other Spanish captains were sent to look into parts of the South American mainland. Spain would not give attention to northern coasts of America for almost another generation.

The Modern Age began with the extension of royal absolutism overseas. The crowns gave patents to individuals to discover, take possession, and govern islands or mainland, inhabited or uninhabited. The crown took to itself the title to land and people, first claimed for it by formal act. Thus Columbus planted the flag as he landed, the natives being bemused spectators. Thus Cabot without having sight of a native. Thus Juan de la Cosa entered on his map the flags of three nations. The course of colonial empire began with disregard of native rights and persons. The Portuguese loaded the first cargo of black slaves when they reached the Bay of Arguin, and they did the same with Indians in Newfoundland. Columbus estimated the prospects of slave trade when he landed in the West Indies. The colonial idea as it took shape in the fifteenth century was untroubled by any concern other than to establish priority over other European nations.

# CHAPTER IV    WHALING AND
# SEA FISHERIES

## *START OF THE NEWFOUNDLAND FISHERIES*

By tradition, as held in Brittany and Normandy, fishing craft went to Newfoundland before the accredited discoverers did so. These richest of fishing grounds are known to have been visited since early in the sixteenth century by an annual swarm of fishing boats from England, Normandy, Brittany, the Basque coast, and Portugal. They came to take cod, especially by fishing alongshore. They had their accustomed landing places, beaches and coves where they dried their catch, mended their gear and boats, supplied themselves with fresh water and firewood, and netted capelins, a smelt-like fish, very abundant and good bait for cod. Fishing continued for many years before there was settlement. Bays and capes became known by proper names, as Cape Race and Bonavista Bay. Biggar thought that such Portuguese place names dated from the time of the Corte Real voyages, which is plausible, since Portuguese fishing boats may well have carried seamen who had been with one of the Corte Real brothers. What of other names, such as Cape Breton? Uncertain traditions have laid claim also to Breton discovery of the newfound lands.

Except for Bristol the records give little support to such claims of discovery by fishermen. That ships went from Bristol to Canadian shores before Cabot has been established, as presented above. Its port register of 1481 of two cargoes of salt seems to imply that such fishing grounds were known by then. It thus appears likely that Bristol was trafficking to Canadian shores by about 1480. Also, the word went out that Bristol men were in search of the island of Brasil.

Bretons appeared early in the Newfoundland fisheries. On the return from the voyage of 1497 Cabot put in at a port in Brittany, which may thus have heard of the new fishing grounds. They may have been known earlier. Fishermen from the Gulf of St. Malo were accustomed to meet and mingle with those from Bristol Channel in the shoal waters south of Ireland. What was known in Bristol was likely to be known in the ports of Brittany. Breton fishermen, well accustomed to the high seas, might be expected to try out the promise of the new waters. By good fortune port records are known of Bristol; for Brittany they are missing.

Portuguese cod fishing in American waters was going on strongly enough by 1506 to attract the attention of the crown. It learned that in Entre Douro e Minho, as the northernmost province was called, judges of the customs had been dispensing tithing rights on "the fish that come from Terra Nova." Because this was a "matter of great importance," such collections were ordered taken over by officers of the King.[1] At that time therefore fishing boats from such places as Porto and Viana do Castelo were making the annual two-thousand-mile trip to take cod off Newfoundland, as they continue to do today.

Could the fishermen of northern Portugal have learned of the Newfoundland cod fishery from the Corte Real voyages of 1501 and 1502? They had previously been engaged in netting small fish in small boats close to shore. Cod were found in cold northern sea, and taken by hook and line. This was a quite different enterprise that needed ample and seaworthy ships to cross the ocean, carrying a sizable crew

[1] Biggar, Doc. 28.

provisioned for months. It required different fishing skills and gear. It required knowing how to prepare and store the dried cod. As with the Bretons, it is not known when or how the Portuguese first began cod fishing across the northern sea.

The Basques were bold navigators, but claims that they discovered Newfoundland are mistaken, as Fernández de Navarrete showed early in the past century and Fernández Duro did later, the two being the old masters of Spanish maritime history. The surprising thing is rather that the Basques were so late in getting to Newfoundland, since they were most active merchants of salt cod and the chief whalers of the time.

Would Juan de la Cosa, for example, have failed to take notice of Spanish priority on Newfoundland shores? He was advisor to the Spanish Crown on affairs of maritime discovery. He took time out from his voyagings to make his famous map, on which he planted English flags along the Canadian coast. Cosa was well informed of Basque sailing. A native of Santoña, an Asturian port on the Basque border, he had learned navigation there, and had laid the foundations of his fortune in Biscayan waters.

Spanish archives record the country's delayed entry to the new found lands. The relevant documents are dated October 1511 and February 1512 and concern a Catalan named Juan de Agramonte.[2] These are reissues of a license given by Philip I, who died in 1506. Agramonte was authorized to go at his own expense to a certain new land that lay within the limits belonging to Spain. (The limits had been set by the Treaty of Tordesillas and in reality lay well to the east of Newfoundland. The license to Agramonte was in effect a challenge of the English title.) The license of Philip

[2] Colección de Documentos Inéditos, vol. 32, pp. 360–361 and 400–401; vol. 39, pp. 402 ff.

58

reads: "The ships and men are to be from my realm, except for two pilots whom you may take who are to be Bretons or of some other nation who may have been there." After going to Brittany, where wine and flour were to be taken, the ships were to sail by way of Galicia. In the renewal of 1511 the destination was given as "Isla de Bacallaos, also called Tierra Nueva." In the document of 1512 it was noted that two Indians in the possession of Agramonte differed from those of Española (Haiti), and also that persons who had been to the new land did not find it as the Portuguese had described it. There is no record that the expedition took place; apparently it did not get beyond the stage of a project.

These licenses show that as late as 1512 Spain had not been in contact with the "new found land," Tierra Nueva. The ships were to proceed from ports of eastern Asturias, adjacent to the Spanish Basque coast. Ships and crew were to be from the Spanish realm which, in terms of ports of departure, indicated Asturians and Basques. It would be necessary to secure pilots from another nation who had been to the new land, also known as Isla de Bacallaos, and to that end Breton pilots should be sought. The original instructions were given by 1506, perhaps the year before, and establish Breton acquaintance with the "new land" at that time, named Bacallaos in the renewal of 1511. By 1512 Agramonte had somehow come into possession of two Indians from those parts who differed from those of the West Indies; it was also known from persons who had been to the new land that it was unlike its Portuguese description. From whom the Indians and information were secured is not stated.

At any rate Spain by 1506 was interested in asserting its papal title to the "new land." In 1512, it still lacked pilots who knew how to get there. The title was to be established against Portugal; England was known to have a claim through Cabot. Bretons would be enlisted to show the way. Then and for years thereafter the designation of the "new found land" of the north was not restricted to the island of Newfoundland but was applied to mainland shores, perhaps as far south as New England.

Cold Labrador lay to the north, of lesser attraction for fishing. Cod drew fishermen from England, Brittany, Portugal, Normandy, and the Basque coast, perhaps in that order, some before and others after the Cabot discovery, commuting across the Atlantic each summer. When fishing extended to the banks from inshore waters is not of record. No settlements were made, nor was there concern to find out what lay inland. The men engaged were not inclined, by literacy or interest, to keep journals. Casual bits of information in official records tell the little that we know.

## NORTHERN LANDS IN THE HIGH MIDDLE AGES

The fifteenth century saw western Europe oriented toward the western ocean because of trade, national power, and curiosity. For the three centuries that went before, the northern ocean remained in dim background. During two of them the Western nations were engaged in Eastern crusades, joining their forces and fortunes to retake the Holy Sepulcher and drive back the infidel Saracen. Most of the crusaders went overland, afoot and on horseback through Italy and the Balkans. Some came by ship out of the north and stopped to give aid to the Portuguese against the Moors. At home the religious mood and aspirations expressed themselves in the wonderful flowering of Gothic architecture. Cities were built to serve industry and commerce, most particularly in Flanders, where Hanseatic and Italian trade met and crafts of high skill developed. Atlantic and Mediterranean lands became linked in various ways in a community of faith, art, industry, and commerce. Mainly it was a time of increased communication of ideas and goods between northwest and south, a time of cultural continentality. Geographical curiosity was not a marked trait of those middle centuries. Marco Polo, their greatest traveler, was little appreciated until late in the fifteenth century. An astronomer friar at Oxford composed the *Inventio Fortunata* around 1350, dealing with the far northern sea and its lands, ostensibly from the 54th degree to the pole. We know of the treatise indirectly from later times, as in the request by the Admiral of Spain to John Day for a copy to be brought from England. Mercator used a version that he found in the Low Countries. Hakluyt cited another in his *Principal Navigations*. We know that the friar knew the use of astrolabes, thought there was a magnetic mountain near the pole (deviation of the compass?), had heard of dangerous whirlpools, and identified Arctic islands. Probably it was a compilation of real and fabulous information on high latitudes rather than the result of his own observations. The *Inventio* fell into neglect, and the few copies made are lost.

The *King's Mirror* was written about 1250 by an unknown Norwegian. Nansen quoted freely from it and considered it as beyond comparison the most important geographical writing on the medieval north, informed, inclusive, and sober. The description included Ireland, Iceland, and Greenland but did not extend farther west. Marine life was well observed, twenty-one kinds of whales (most of them valid) were noted, six of seals, the walrus, and so on. The *King's Mirror* was concerned with the Norse parts of the north and was little known beyond Scandinavia.

A commercial geography of Atlantic Europe in the Middle Ages remains to be written which will inform of the kinds and places of primary commodities, of the manner of their assembly and transport, of their processing, and of their ultimate destinations. The trade overland between

61

Flanders and Italian cities is well known, as is the net of intermediate inland cities. The counters at which the Hanse collected fish, wool and hides, timber and pitch about the North and Baltic seas are well documented, but not so their first sources and final distributions. Little has been done on the overland transport of goods between Biscayan and Catalonian ports over the shortest passage between the Atlantic and Mediterranean.

From the Bay of Biscay to the north of the Norwegian Sea the ocean was harvested continuously and increasingly far out into the high sea. During the high Middle Ages a major business developed in the supply of fish and whale products to inland markets and also to Mediterranean Europe. Fishermen and sea hunters of different nations became well and widely familiar with northern seas. Their products were a major stimulus to the rise of inland cities and furnished a staple food for the people of central and southern Europe. In major outline Fritz Bartz has sketched this early commercial fishing, tracing the fishing grounds and their seasons and describing the skills of procuring and processing.[3] This commerce required converting the catch to durable products that could be stored and carried to distant markets. Atlantic fishing and whaling in this period was joined to the building of more seaworthy and versatile ships, the training of mariners and merchants on certain parts of the Atlantic coast, the growth of greater confidence to fare wherever there was promise of reward for whatever the length of the voyage.

## BISCAYAN BACALAO, WHALES, AND NAVAL ENGAGEMENT

Throughout the Mediterranean salt-dried codfish is known as *bacalao* and is made into locally esteemed dishes. The product comes from northern seas and was taken to

[3] Bartz, vol. 1, pp. 70–83.

southern markets in a medieval trade in which mainly the Basques were involved. Salt cod formed a major item in a commerce that can be traced back to the twelfth century. It modified the food habits of southern Europe and later of slave plantations in the New World. It brought fishing fleets of a half-dozen European nations annually to North American waters throughout the sixteenth century. The topic is in need of study.

The cod and its kindred, ling, haddock, and pollack, are the major game fish of the cold waters of the Northern Atlantic. As predators, they follow the small surface-feeding fish that seek out the plankton-rich tracts in seasonal movements. Feeding and especially spawning take place in the shallow coastal waters and on shoal banks out at sea. The cod fishing grounds extend from the southern side of the Bay of Biscay through the North and Norwegian seas, around the British Isles and Faeroes to Iceland, but the greatest massing is off Newfoundland, Nova Scotia, and south to and beyond Cape Cod.

Cod were taken by baited hooks, at first by hand lines, then by long-lining, a series of hooks hanging from a long line supported by floats. (In the American vernacular of river fishing this is known as running a trot line or jugging.) Abundant bait was necessary, usually the meat of shellfish or netted small fish.[4] Dory-like small boats were and are an important adjunct to cod fishing.

The commercial advantages of cod are numerous. At the proper place and season they can be found in enormous numbers. They grow to good size, to 20 pounds and more in weight. The fish is easily split and cleaned and, being of lean flesh, can be dried without turning rancid. The split

---

[4] One of the advantages of the Newfoundland fishery has been the abundance inshore of capelin, of the smelt family (also found in the fjords of Iceland).

fish, freely exposed to the air and salted, may be kept indefinitely. Preserving methods differed, but salt was generally used. Curing required none of the laborious steps—careful smoking, pickling, and packing in casks—that herring, mackerel, and other oily fish did. The preparation could be done on shipboard. If a landing place was available the split fish were hung by their tails on stakes (whence the northern term stockfish) until sufficiently dried, after which they were stacked like boards, more salt being added. No other fish was as easy to prepare and transport, none excelled it in food value, and none was considered its equal in taste.

The Basques are credited with having begun the commercial cod fishery. They and their Asturian neighbors developed a market for bacalao around and across the Mediterranean. The usual and principal argument for their priority, however—that the product carries a Basque name—is insecure. Wherever the fishermen of a country began to take the fish, they gave it a name of local language. In English this is *cod*, in Norse *torsk*, in German *Dorsch*, in French *morue*, in Spanish *abadejo*. The commercial product was given a different name. This is *stokkfisk* in Norse and *stockfish* in English, a name which later fell into disuse. In Spain and Portugal it is *bacalao/bacallao/bacalhao*. The Portuguese probably borrowed the name from their neighbors when they took to fishing northern waters.

North of the Basques, in France, the Low Countries, Germany, and into Denmark a curious metathesis occurred between *bacalao* and *cabillaud* or *kabeljau*. *Cabillaud* is documented from France in 1278, *cabellauw* from Flanders in 1163.[5] Dried cod is thus of earliest record in Flanders, then the hub of trade by land and sea. The name *kabeljau* does not sound Germanic, nor was Hanseatic commerce as much

[5] J. Corominas, *Diccionario Critico*, under bacalao.

concerned with it, as Bascayan commerce was. One name with minor variations is used in Germanic, Romance, and Basque languages. It would be interesting to know about Breton. If it should be known where the term originated, the origin of this commercial fishery might be located.[6]

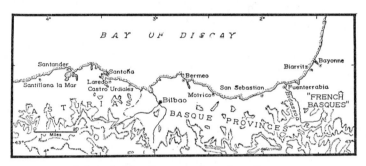

Map 6. The Basque-Asturian Coast.

Basques and eastern Asturians or Montañeses shared the inner part of the Bay of Biscay (map 6). The Basques have lived there from time immemorial, aboriginal occupants of the western Pyrenees and of the coast west beyond Bilbao. The Montañeses, neighbors to the west, are the people of the province of Santander, between the Cantabrian Mountains and the Bay of Biscay, the Picos de Europa their south-western boundary. They are part of Old Castile, land of Visigothic conquest, known in the high Middle Ages as Asturias de Santillana. Santillana la Mar today is a small town noted for the caves of Altamira and the medieval town houses of Castilian nobles. These Castilian-speaking people, adjoining the Basques to the east, appear under the name of Old Castilian, Asturian, or Biscayan (Vizcaino), the latter also applying to Basques. The two peoples, greatly

[6] Capelin, the usual bait for cod in Newfoundland, is said to be derived from French *capelan* (chaplain). The reason is not apparent. Might it not be linked to cabillaud/capellaud?

65

differing in language and social structure, were closely associated in maritime enterprise.

The Biscayan land, sloping northward from mountains to bay, knows no season of drought and little of cold or heat. It had forests of oak and pine, pastures and meadows, and many arable tracts. A green and pleasant land, it developed good husbandry and a numerous population. Beds of iron ore supported an early industry in metallurgy. The sea coast, fretted by rocky headlands and sheltered bays, gave access to the harvest of abundant marine life and to the open and notoriously rough Bay of Biscay. Inland, ancient land routes lead across gaps in the Cantabrian Mountains to the meseta of Old Castile and especially to the Ebro valley and thus to Catalonia and the Mediterranean. Both peoples took early advantage of location and resource of land and sea.

It was only this eastern third of the north coast of Spain that developed maritime activities early, as was pointed out by Cesáreo Fernández Duro.[7] Galicia, like Portugal, was notoriously laggard in getting onto the high seas, until long after the Biscayan coast was busied with fishing, hunting whales, building ships, and commerce. The history of the coast of Santander was the theme of the last study by Don Antonio Ballesteros y Beretta, *La Marina Cantabra y Juan de la Cosa* (Santander, 1964), concluding with the career of its most famous native son. There is no comparable study of the Basque coast to the east. The hundred miles of coast from Santillana to Fuenterrabia on Rio Bidassoa at the boundary with France hold a neglected chapter of maritime venturing.

Well-endowed monasteries fostered commerce by land and sea early, perhaps before the twelfth century, and were

[7] Fernández Duro, *Disquisiciones Nauticas*, especially vol. 6 (Madrid, 1881).

the beginnings of such towns as Santander, Santoña, and Santillana. San Sebastian on the Basque side was given royal privileges of trade in 1150 and 1202, according to Fernández Duro "one of the oldest codes of maritime trade known." During the twelfth century Biscayan ships traded to Flanders, Normandy, and England. There are records of import of cloth from the north and scantier ones of the export of iron ware and wine (from La Rioja?). Wool and ships were important exports. Spanish trade with northern Europe appears to have been controlled by Biscayan ports well into the sixteenth century. Santander and nearby ports provided ships and crews for the Moorish wars, taking an important part in the capture of Cartagena and Seville (1245 and 1247).

The Hermandad de las Marismas was formed in 1296 by the port towns from Santander to Fuenterrabia, the objective being protection of their sea trade to Flanders, the northern sea passage becoming hazardous as the contest between England and France developed. Instead of keeping aloof, as was the original intention in arming Biscayan ships, these shortly were engaging English vessels. The English Crown complained of piracy by the Hermandad, especially as directed against Bayonne, then belonging to England. When the Hundred Years' War broke out (1337) the Hermandad intervened openly on the French side. Its ships engaged an English fleet in the Strait of Dover at Winchelsea in 1350 and were soundly drubbed. The menace was sufficient to cause Edward III to make a treaty with the Hermandad that ran for twenty years and appears to have been observed. After its expiration the Hermandad was a major naval arm of France. It inflicted a serious defeat on the English fleet before La Rochelle (1372), took part in sacking the Isle of Wight (1374), raided English Channel ports (1377), and sailed up the Thames and burned Gravesend (1380). "The people of the litoral of northern Spain known by the name of Biscayans, intimately united by community enterprise, constituted a powerful naval force, capable of carrying on war with northern powers independently of the kings of Castile, whose intervention was nominal rather than effective."[8]

The Hermandad began as a league for the protection of its trade with Flanders, shortly preyed on English shipping, and passed to warfare against England, in which it was treated as a sovereign power by the English Crown. After the expiration of the treaty it again furnished support to France. It was not warring for Castile, nor because it was attached to the cause of France, nor insofar as is known for fear of England. Probably it profited from the conflict between England and France; the towns belonging to the Hermandad seem to have continued to thrive, to build ships, to go to the high sea for cod and whales, to engage in distant commerce.

Basque tradition holds that its people have taken whales from early times. The Biscayan coast was the southernmost limit to which the black right whales (*Balaena biscayensis*) ranged. In winter they moved south to this region, where calving took place, mothers and young frequenting the sheltered inlets. Was this immemorial seasonal migration watched by Paleolithic artists of Altamira, hoping that a leviathan would strand there? In all Europe the Biscayan coastal waters were frequented most regularly and for the longest time by these whales. How this accessibility was first utilized in hunting by boat and harpoon is unknown. Lesser creatures of the sea were thus taken in classical times in the Mediterranean. Basque ironworkers knew of old the skills of smithing knives, lances, and harpoons, the tools of whaling.

---

[8] Fernández Duro, vol. 6, p. 232.

# WHALING AND SEA FISHERIES

By the time Biscayan towns were being given royal charters in the thirteenth century, whaling was an established business. The privileges granted specified the manner of taking whales, the allocation of the carcass among the participants, and the tribute (commonly the tongue) that pertained to monastery or official. Lookout towers on headlands were manned in season to report the sighting of whales. At least six town seals of the thirteenth and fourteenth centuries figure whales, mainly in the act of being harpooned. Those of Bermeo, Motrico, and Fuenterrabia show a harpooner in an open boat at the side of a whale.[9]

The right whales fed mainly on krill, small crustaceans living on the plant plankton, which the whales strained out through their long baleen plates (whalebone). As the whales moved from one plankton pasture northward to another, they were followed by whalers. The hunting of the right whales had the special advantage that the carcass stayed afloat. In earlier times the procedure was to kill the animal from an open boat and then tow it ashore to be cut up and rendered. Later ships were built that followed the whales at sea. The ship moved up to the carcass, the blubber and meat were sliced off and loaded, and then a landing was sought for the rendering. For an unknown but probably lengthy period the whalers finished their work on land.

The business was a Basque specialty. Asturians, in other ways their companions at sea, are not reported as thus engaged. Ciriquiain-Gaiztarro reports Basques hunting whales to the west off Asturias and Galicia in the thirteenth century. Nansen cited a document to the effect that merchants of Bayonne in 1202 were making an annual payment for permission to take whales about St. Michel in the Breton Gulf of St. Malo, perhaps a landing rather than hunting per-

<hr>

9 Mariano Ciriquiain-Gaiztarro, *Los Vascos en la Pesca de la Ballena* (San Sebastian, 1961).

Distintos sellos municipales dc Bermeo.

Escudo de Guetaria

Escudo de Ondárroa

Escudo de Motrico

Sello de Fuenterrabía del año 1297

Escudo de Lequeitio

Basque Town Seals Showing Whales (Ciriquiain-Gaiztarro).

70

mit. Bayonne, then in English possession, was French Basque country. The document is of interest as to the distance ships were going from the inner part of the Bay of Biscay in pursuit of whales.

The chief product was whale oil, which required containers for which the Basque forests of oaks and pines provided cooperage, as they did for the wine that they carried north. Trying out blubber required wood fuel only at the start. Once the process had begun the rendered residue kept the fire going. How long it took before whale oil was tried out on shipboard instead of on shore appears not to be known.[10] It would have been a small matter to seat the caldrons on a fireproof hearth on shipboard, thus freeing the ships from the necessity of hunting a landing place whenever they took a whale. It seems reasonable to infer that when the ships turned from coastal to pelagic whaling they also began to render blubber on board. It may also be surmised that bacalao was prepared at the same time. Right whale and cod frequented the same plankton grounds. While waiting to make the great kill the men could drop lines to catch cod, some to feed the crew, others to be split and hung up to dry. Codding and whaling were main Basque activities; they may well have been carried on together, as appears later to have been done off Newfoundland.

Basques developed a broad-beamed ship for whaling, known as *ballener*. According to Ciriquiain-Gaiztarro it was of eighty to a hundred tons, responsive to steering and fast. A stylized reproduction may be represented on the 1297 seal of the town of San Sebastian. The ballener also was employed as a merchant ship. One out from Bilbao was taken by the Portuguese in 1423. Another was recorded as

[10] Ivan Sanderson, *Follow the Whale* (New York, 1956), found no such record until the late sixteenth century.

71

bringing cargo to Bruges in 1449. In England it was known as the *balinger*, the two Bristol ships of the transatlantic voyage of 1481 being such (p. 36).

The great right whale was hunted steadily and in time was destroyed as a commercial resource. Fernández Duro wrote: "Be it by persecution or for other reasons, the appearance of the whales in the Gulf of Cantabria declined steadily until the sight of a single one became an event. In consequence the industry they supported was lost as was the custom of keeping lookouts along the shores."[11] He listed the dates of late single sightings between 1764 and 1854. Since the Bay of Biscay was where they overwintered and calved, a comparable general reduction in numbers is implied. Human predation thus reduced a species of low reproduction almost to extinction in the eastern Atlantic.

These pieces of information fit into a rough pattern and sequence, sufficient to show that the Biscayan coast from Santillana and Santander to Fuenterrabia and across to Bayonne saw major maritime activity at least as far back as the twelfth century. It has had little attention in Spanish or in European history. Castile was fighting Moors and quarreling with Portugal and was about to take the Canary Islands. Aragon was concerned with Catalonia and then with Italy. Even in the early Spanish history of the New World the important Biscayan participation has been scantily noticed. Some of the neglect is due to the marginal association of the Basque provinces with whatever crown was in authority. Some of it comes from the limited preoccupations of political history.

The Biscayan outlook, both of the Basques and the Castilians of eastern Asturias, was to the northern sea. Their land, attractive and varied in its resources, adjoined a sea

[11] Fernández Duro, p. 293.

productive of marine life with a coastline of numerous, good, and sheltered harbors. When faring into the high seas began is not known. By the time that towns were given charters in the twelfth century they were thus engaged, as shown by the maritime code of San Sebastian of 1150. Trade was carried on with the north, especially Flanders, the great entrepôt of Atlantic Europe. South they carried an overland commerce to Catalan ports on the Mediterranean. They built good ships, bred a race of blue water seamen, and developed a merchant class. The Hermandad de las Marismas was in some ways a southern counterpart of the Hanseatic League and acted at times as a sovereign power.

How early the commerce in whale oil and bacalao began is not known. Fernández Duro thought that commercial whaling began before the trade in bacalao. In any case the Biscayan beginnings were learned in their own coastal waters, from which they worked out into the northern seas. The prestige and profit of whale hunting is expressed in the early seals of port towns. The origin of the bacalao trade may hang on determining the origin of the word bacalao/kabeljau. Does the documentation of *kabeljau* in Flanders in 1163 show that Basques introduced dried cod there or that they adopted its northern name?

How far Biscayan ships went into the northern ocean also remains unknown. Their interest was in commerce, in the taking of whales and cod, not in discovery of unknown lands. However far they went they did not discover new land across the sea, nor were they among the first to fish those waters.

## GLOSS ON NORSE WHALING

Nansen liked the idea that Norsemen may have carried the art of harpooning of whales south when they settled in Normandy and that thus Basques may have learned the skill

73

as they came north to the English Channel.[12] Harpooning, however, was known to Europeans long before historical times. It is irrelevant therefore to construe medieval sequence from use of the harpoon by different European nations. The weapon is found archaeologically far antedating a time when one can speak of Germanic or Celtic peoples. In historic times, as Nansen admitted, harpoons were used in hunting seal, walrus, dolphin, and large fish, any large creatures of the sea, from Arctic shores to the Mediterranean.

Whale meat and blubber were appreciated food wherever available, from the Bay of Biscay to the Arctic coasts of Russia. Whales stranded occasionally. They wandered into narrow waters, such as fjords, where they could be hemmed in. Nansen cited a Spanish–Arabic author of the eleventh century on the taking of young whales by Norsemen in Ireland. The droll details are fantastically distorted; the manner of separating the calf from its mother, pulling the carcass to shore, and cutting up and salting of the flesh apply as well to others than Norse. The reduction of the once abundant right whales may well have begun by the killing of the young, easiest to take and most desirable as to flesh. The Arabic tale about Ireland does indicate wide and early communication of knowledge of the sea in northern lands.

A footnote by Nansen[13] raises the question, unnoticed by him, of early Celtic whaling and its possible connection with Basques. The document referred to is dated 832 and relates to the parish of Coutances in western Normandy on the Gulf of St. Malo. It predates the Norman conquest, the population being mainly Celtic. The coast of Coutances is only a few miles north of that of St. Michel, to which Bay-

---

[12] Nansen, vol. 2, esp. pp. 148–164.
[13] Nansen, vol. 2, p. 159.

onne was paying an annual rental for whaling rights in 1202. The early connections of Basques and Bretons have been very little explored. We do not know when Basques first came as whalers to Breton shores. We do not know whether they knew the preparation of bacalao and taught it to Bretons or whether the reverse was the case.

Right and other whales were hunted by Norse along Norwegian shores and to some extent off Ireland, Iceland, and Greenland. They made an occasional welcome addition of red meat and blubber to the diet. It is likely that some whale oil was processed and shipped, but it is not recorded that this was done regularly or in the amount that seal oil was. There is no record of a commerce such as the Basques carried on, or of ships designed for and engaged in the business of whaling. The data Nansen collected are of the viking period and are incidental to their seafaring for loot, conquest, and colonization, and they refer to local consumption of whale meat. It is only by uncertain inference that such activity extended to pursuit of whales on the high seas. After viking times (after the eleventh century) Norse seafaring declined rapidly. The Norse ceased to be warriors of the sea, nor did they learn to be its merchants or shippers. By the seventeenth century Peder Clausson Friis wrote of hunting whales as a dim memory: "In ancient times many expedients or methods were used for catching whales . . . but on account of men's unskillfulness they have fallen out of use, so that they now have no means of hunting the whale unless he drifts ashore to them."

Basques continued to hunt and process whales, as they did bacalao. They became a nation of shipbuilders, navigators, and merchants, and later of industrialists and bankers. The continuity is unbroken from the eleventh century to the present. Bretons were also involved early, the manner and time remaining obscure. Norse seamanship, supreme when they went out as vikings, fell off abruptly thereafter, and was of little significance in the commerce of the North Atlantic.

## THE HERRING FISHERIES

Commercial herring fishing may have begun in the eleventh century. As the most abundant and most widely ranging northern fish, it was available in great quantity in many places. The North Sea and the channels that lead to it have been its prime fishing grounds. All coastal waters about the North and Norwegian seas as well as the sea corridor from Scotland by way of the Shetland and Faeroe islands to Iceland are highly productive. Herring move in schools, feeding in waters rich in plankton and seeking shoals for spawning. At the time of the spawning runs they are mature, gravid with roe and milt, in prime condition, in large assembly, and in accessible locations in shoal coast waters and on submarine banks. It is of first importance to fishermen to know the pattern and calendar of this circulation of schools, which continues throughout the year.

The fish, being small and oily, are more difficult to prepare for keeping than cod. One means is by drying over a smoky fire. The term kipper was originally applied to salmon, a prized freshwater fish of the early Low German peoples, and may suggest that the process was transferred to herring. Salting, such as pickling in brine, was more costly, salt being an item that had to be purchased. Usually the herring were packed in casks for preservation and transport.

For a time the herring fishery was carried on by nets set in shoal waters, as in estuaries at time of spawning runs. The fishermen used rowboats and took the catch to their village, where it was cleaned by the women and children and then processed and packed. The product was bought by merchant shippers, mostly from other parts. Such was the beginning of the Hanseatic herring trade. Villagers along the sounds that connect the North and Baltic seas, both on the Swedish and Danish side, procured and processed the fish. Hanse ships, especially from Lubeck, bought them and supplied salt. On the English coast of the North Sea the development was similar, fishing places in number growing into commercial port towns.

The next step was to follow the school as it moved at sea. This was done by ships carrying a large net with floats, with small boats in tow. Such drift nets were thrown out overnight across the course of a school moving on its circuit of feeding or spawning. The ships could go as far and stay out at sea as long as the catch would keep under preliminary salting. Ships from England, Scotland, the Low Countries, and Scandinavia congregated on banks in the North Sea and in other waters distant from their homes, as did others from southwest England, Brittany, and Normandy in the shoal waters south of Ireland and on the English Channel. Fishermen of different nations shared the waters amicably and commonly were permitted to use foreign ports, at least on the English coast, to complete the job of processing. Great Yarmouth, for example, long the first herring port of the North Sea, thus assigned parts of its waterfront to foreign fishermen.

The station of herring fishing in Atlantic annals is humble. Its fishermen discovered no unknown islands or seas, nor did they contribute names to history. The herring fishery bred its yeomen of the sea, self-reliant, giving mutual aid, and risking their persons and property to frequent and sudden hazards. North Sea and English Channel trained a race of seamen, apprenticed by fishing. The commerce in herring contributed to the rise of a merchant class and the building of ships. With the decline of the Hanse and the drain and destruction of the Hundred Years' War, most serious in Normandy and Brittany but also in Flanders, the Dutch entered on their maritime period, largely through the herring trade. They built superior ships and introduced better means of curing and grading fish, which soon gave the Dutch product preference on the continental market. The fifteenth century was the beginning of the seaward orientation of the Dutch by which they were to move later to far seas.

# CHAPTER V   THE VIKINGS

## VIKING WAYS

The Scandinavian sea raiders, who called themselves vikings, began their invasions abroad late in the eighth century, terrorized Atlantic Europe through the ninth, and gave up their wild way during the tenth. In the western sea they were Norsemen and Danes, joined by some Swedes and Goths. They attacked settlements along the coasts and also rowed their ships up rivers, even entering the Mediterranean Sea as far as Italy.

It was a barbaric society gone to extremes in prizing valor. Their sagas are filled with violence at home, with casual or intended affronts that resulted in quick killings and were followed by long blood feuds. Brawl or battle, they were ready to fight and to die as the gods expected. Thor, the youthful god of thunder and hammer, was their special patron. They sacrificed to him and gave his name to their sons. Thor approved of men who sought danger and risked their lives in battle. Vikings served a cult of combat that gave distinction to the brave and rewarded the victor with the goods and persons of the vanquished. The Norse sagas celebrated as great vikings men who adhered to the pagan faith, leaders by right of their ability to command. Viking ways declined when central rule was established and died out as Christianity replaced the Nordic gods.

Christian Europe had not seen the like of these wild men who came raging out of the north, even their ships striking fear with their figureheads of dragons and serpents.

Surprise and terror were main viking weapons. The ships were designed for attack. High of prow and stern and slender in waist, they sailed smartly with the wind. A bank of oars, served in shifts of rowers, gave the means to go ahead when wind failed and also to enter estuaries and tidal rivers. The viking party was commanded by a chieftain, its members were his kinsmen, their thanes and thralls, a feudality transferred to sea, a well-organized and highly mobile striking force. A common tactic was to seize a small island and from this base to plunder the countryside at leisure. The northmen were equipped with superior arms, strange to the invaded people, double-edged broadswords, double-bitted battle-axes, tall hide-covered shields, head and body armor, all meant for hand-to-hand conflict.

For a time the vikings were content to attack and sack and then return home with loot and captives. Success gave prestige and wealth at home. The erstwhile head of a small district on a Norwegian fjord, thus possessed of foreign treasure, acquired a larger following, authority, and domain. His success moved others to try their fortunes. The local aristocracy became more stratified, and some of its lords, grown great, were known in the chronicles as kings. In time viking chieftains, attracted by the more genial lands where they plundered and found the defenses of the inhabitants weak, turned to conquest and settlement overseas. Thus the Frankish–Celtic land on the English Channel which they had ravaged repeatedly in the ninth century became the Duchy of Normandy of the Dane Rollo and his Norse following. Viking migration overseas became a major exodus in the latter part of the ninth century, when Harald Fair Hair made himself lord of all Norway. Many vikings, resenting the loss of their own absolute freedom, got out with dependents and possessions.

Southwest Norway was the greatest center of dispersal

overseas (map 7). Here the highland, largely of rock bared
by glaciation, abuts upon the ocean in a series of prom-
ontories and fjorded valleys, long and many-branched. The
lower parts of the fjords are deeply submerged, their flanks
rock-walled. Arable land and meadows are mainly found inland on and about the heads of fjords. This Norwegian fjord

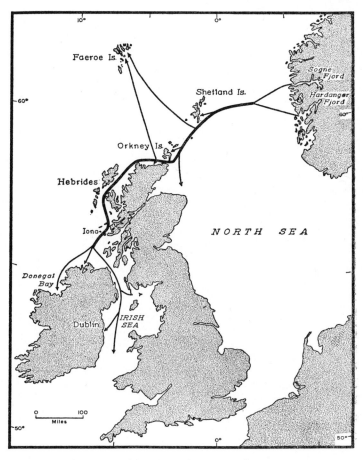

Map 7. Dispersal of Vikings from Southwestern Norway.

country restricts settlement to narrow strips, branching inland from sheltered sounds. Good plowland is in short supply, meadow and pasture somewhat less so. The seasons of good harvest of field and meadow are uncertain. Fishing in and beyond the fjords supplemented the laborious husbandry. What was gained was shared with the rustic lords. In time there were more people than found sustenance. From the great Hardanger and Sogne fjords an emigration went to better and ampler lands overseas, and became a formidable stream in the latter ninth century when Harald's new order took effect. The vikings who would not knuckle under took their ships, families, and dependents to claim new homes.

## VIKINGS TO THE BRITISH ISLES

In the late eighth century vikings began to raid the Shetland and Orkney islands.[1] Before the end of the century they were pillaging the north coast of Scotland, the sacred isle of Iona, the Hebrides, the Bay of Dublin, and South Wales. The seaway around northern Britain and into the Irish Sea continued throughout the ninth century to be the main route of viking penetration. By 825 they were making inroads well into Ireland.

Ireland, like Normandy somewhat later, was a great prize to be taken. It was prosperous, advanced in crafts and learning beyond other northern lands, in full flowering of Christian civilization. Its castles, churches, monasteries, and towns yielded rich booty, such as gold, then produced and worked in quantity on the island. The countryside was fair beyond anything the men of the narrow Norse fjords had known, scarcely touched by cold of winter, lush of meadow and pasture, and with much good plowland. Northmen who came to plunder stayed to dispossess the Irish gentry.

The viking migration increased after Harald Fair Hair

[1] Gwyn Jones, *The North Atlantic Saga* (London, 1964), p. 18.

imposed his order to Norway and extended it to the Shetlands and Orkneys in 875. Meanwhile Irish chieftains were
raising resistance to the usurpers to push them back to the
comparative security of the coast. Dublin was retaken from
the Norse in 902.

The relations between the two peoples were not always
hostile. The Northmen were in short supply of women and
seized or wooed Irish girls of high as well as low degree.
Whether or not the bonds were solemnized by the Church,
the women remained Christian and the children were most
likely to be thus reared. Their Irish kindred found some acceptance among the Norse. Some of the vikings were becoming Christianized. An acculturation had begun in which
the higher Irish culture was to prevail again. The Norse were
beginning to merge with the Irish, and others were being
pushed out of territory they had taken. The prospects of a
Norse Ireland faded, lacking a Rollo to organize them into

Dragon Ship with King and Warrior, from *Flateyjarbok*
(Nansen).

a cohesive militant aristocracy. Elsewhere about the British Isles they fared no better, except in the Orkneys and Shetlands, where Harald was in control.

Those who would still be vikings, free of an overlord, began to look elsewhere for seats. The one direction that was left open was the north. These were no longer the vikings of old going out to battle and plunder. They would take along their kinsmen, thanes, and thralls, some of the latter being Irish slaves, but they would be content to find homes where they could live by husbandry. This final retreat into the northern wilderness had its point of departure from the British Isles as well as from Harald's Norway.

## OCCUPATION OF THE FAEROE ISLANDS

The Faeroe Islands, rough volcanic hills and mountains (map 8) lie about two hundred miles northwest of the Shetlands, a little farther north from the extremity of Scotland. They were known before the vikings took to sea. Dicuil, learned Irish monk at the Carolingian court, was first to mention them in writing. His treatise will be noted later. The immediate concern is to place the islands in their Norse context. Dicuil finished his book in 825, perhaps at Aachen. He had been living for some years on the continent, one of numerous Irish monks engaged there in teaching. Whether he brought his information on the northern sea from his earlier life in Ireland or had it from Irish monks who came later is not stated.

Map 8. Faeroe Islands.

# THE VIKINGS

Dicuil knew that the Faeroe Islands were being visited by Norse brigands (in his Latin, *latron*), who caused the Irish occupants to evacuate them. He did not say that vikings had then settled in them, as has been construed in error by some commentators. At the beginning of the ninth century vikings were coursing widely from the Shetlands along Scottish coasts into Ireland, but they had not begun to settle the Faeroes. Dicuil records only that at that time vikings had been to the Faeroes and had caused the Irish monks who lived there to abandon them.

The Norse Saga of the Faeroes (*Faereyingasaga*) begins:

> There was a man named Grim Kamban. He was the first to settle on the Faeroes in the days of Harald Fair Hair. At that time many fled the king's seeking of power. Many came to live in the Faeroes and built their homesteads there; some fared on to other uninhabited islands. Aud the Deep-Minded, on her way to Iceland, came to the Faeroes and married off Aloef, daughter of Thorstein the Red, and from her is descended the noblest lineage of the Faeroes.

The saga dates the Norse occupation of the Faeroes at the time of the great viking exodus to escape the rule of Harald in Norway, the Shetlands, and Orkneys, which was at the beginning of the last quarter of the ninth century. It also tells of Norse who came from the British Isles, with special pride in the lineage of Aud the Deep-Minded, famed in Icelandic sagas. Aud was the widow of Olaf, King of Dublin, who fell in battle in Ireland. She then moved to the Hebrides with her son Thorstein the Red, who was killed in fighting on the Scottish mainland. With her following and Thorstein's progeny she came to the Faeroes, there to marry off granddaughters before taking up her final home in Iceland. The Norse settlement of the Faeroes began at about the same time as that of Iceland and for the same reason of finding land beyond the control of Harald. Toward the end of the century other vikings and their dependents came from

85

the British Isles to get away from the increasingly formidable natives.

The Faeroes Saga continues by telling how some of the settlers became prosperous squires on several islands and others went out to take part in fighting in Norway and elsewhere. The Faeroes had attraction for homeseekers. The newcomers found a number of the islands well stocked with sheep that had continued to thrive in that extraordinarily mild climate after the Irish had left. There were great rookeries of seafowl and seals and abundance of fish. The islands were a convenient way station between Norway, Iceland, and Britain. The scores of islands, not all habitable, comprise little more than five hundred square miles, unsuited to tillage and used only in part for pasture. The resource of the land shortly was fully employed.

## NORSE RECONNAISSANCE OF ICELAND

The Norse discovery of Iceland is attributed to three viking voyages in the decade of 860, remembered in the Icelandic sagas.[2] The first voyage is attributed to Gardar Svavarsson, a Swedish viking who had been living in Norway. He set out to lay claim to an inheritance in the Hebrides that belonged to his wife, was caught in a storm that carried

---

[2] The old Icelandic literature is accessible in various translations that are in good agreement. The two great sources on early Icelandic are the *Islendigabok*, written by Ari Thorgilsson the Learned, and the *Landnamabok*, of which he may also have been an author. The first is sober history, careful of time and persons, the second a gazetteer of the subdivision of Iceland among the pioneer families, about four hundred of whom are named and located as to their holdings and how these were acquired. Both were written in the twelfth century to preserve knowledge that had been passed orally for centuries. Two versions of the *Landnamabok* are known, one of the *Sturlubok* of the thirteenth century, the other the *Hauksbok* of the fourteenth, differing in some details but hardly in disagreement. A late English rendering of the sources is Gwyn Jones, *The Norse Atlantic Saga*, with basic bibliography. The German series, *Thule*, edited by Felix Niedner, has a good discussion of physical and cultural geography in early Norse time, entitled *Islands Besiedlung und älteste Geschichte* (Jena, 1928), vol. 23.

him northwest far off his course, and made land in south-eastern Iceland (map 9). From here he followed the south coast, cliff-flanked and nearly harborless, and so came to the broad fjords of the west, then continued around the north coast, overwintering at Husavik, "house bay," still so called from the shelter he built. On completing the circuit of the island he returned to Norway, praising the land he had found and calling it Gardarsholm after himself.

The next discoverer was Naddod the Viking. "He was a great viking, who went off to make a home for himself in the Faeroes for the good reason that he had nowhere else where he would be safe" (*Hauksbok*). A troublesome character apparently, who sought safety in the distant Faeroes. The statement neither proves or disproves that the Faeroes were then inhabited by Norse. He too missed his objective but was "sea-tossed to Gardarsholm" (*Hauksbok*), also

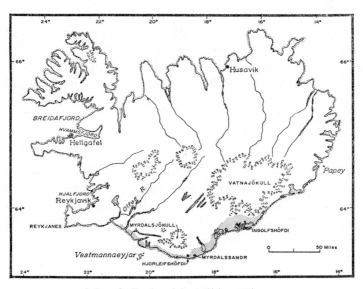

Map 9. Iceland in Viking Time.

landing on the southeast coast. He climbed up a mountain to see whether there was any sign of people but found none. As they left a heavy snow fell in the mountains, for which reason they called the island Snaeland. They made their return by way of the Faeroes (*Sturlubok*) and praised the land highly.

The third voyager, Floki Vilgerdarson, was also called a great viking. He set out with the intention of settling in Gardarsholm, taking with him his family and cattle. One of the party was a Hebridean (Norse or Celt?). Before leaving Norway Floki made a great sacrifice and hallowed three ravens "to guide him on his way, for in those days sailors in the Northlands had no loadstone" (*Hauksbok*). He sailed first to the Shetlands, where one daughter lost her life, and then to the Faeroes, where a second daughter found a husband. On leaving the Faeroes he released the first raven, which flew back to land. The second flew high into the air and then returned to the ship. The third flew straight ahead in the direction where they found land, again at the southeast end of Iceland. They followed the route Gardar had taken along the forbidding south shore and got to the great embayment of Breidafjord at the west, finding the entire fjord full of fish and seals. They spent so much time fishing and hunting here that they neglected to put up hay for their cattle, all of which died during the winter. For winter quarters they built a hall and boat house on the northern (Bardarstrand) shore of Breidafjord. In the spring Floki walked north to a mountain from which he could see the sea to the north full of ice drift. For this reason he named the land Iceland. When he got back to Norway Floki gave it a bad name, but one of his companions said that butter dripped there from every blade of grass, thus recommending it as a future dairy country.

Gardar had been on his way to the Hebrides, Naddod to the Faeroes when they were storm-driven far out of their course, as would happen again and again in later times in these seas. Gardar was checking on an inheritance, Naddod was ducking vengeance, and Floki had daughters to marry off on his way to the land Gardar had found and recommended. All three landed in the southeastern fjords. Gardar and Floki took their course along the south coast, of grim basalt cliffs and strands of shifting dunes, and got to the wide bays and fjords of the west, the most attractive part of the island. They experienced a winter longer and colder than in their Norwegian home, saw the ice floes that drifted out of the Arctic to the north coast, and knew the land to be covered with stunted scrub and with moors. The name that survived, Iceland, gave notice that this would not be a land of easy and generous rewards.

## FIRST SETTLERS OF ICELAND

The first step toward the occupation of Iceland was taken in 870 by the foster brothers Ingolf and Leif, the latter later called Hjorleif. The story, told at some length in *Landnamabok*, illustrates how vikings fell to quarreling and what might happen to the losers. The locale was Dalsfjord, next north of Sognefjord in southwest Norway. One kindred held the upper part of the fjord, that of the foster brothers the part toward the sea. Both groups had joined in viking raids, later fell out, and had taken to fighting, as the result of which the foster brothers agreed to surrender their estates. Ingolf and Leif then fitted out a large ship "to seek the land that Raven Floki had found." They spent the winder of 870 in the eastern fjords of Iceland and returned to Norway.

While Ingolf collected their capital to return to Iceland, Leif went on a viking expedition to Ireland. There he entered a large house underground, dark until he saw it lit up from a sword in the hand of a man, whom he killed. He then took the sword and great riches, and thereafter was known as Hjorleif (Sword Leif). The *Landnamabok* continues that he plundered far and wide in Ireland, gained great riches, captured ten thralls, and returned to Norway. "That winter Ingolf offered great sacrifice and sought auguries, but Hjorleif would never sacrifice." (Ingolf was true to the old gods; Hjorleif had seen Irish Christianity and may have acquired some doubts.) Hjorleif put his booty on his ship, Ingolf loaded their common stock on his. And so they set out for Iceland in 874.

In the first settlement of Iceland good judgment played no part. As in the previous cases the approach was at the southeastern end. As soon as land was sighted Ingolf "cast overboard the pillars of his high seat for good omen, vowing that he would settle wherever they came ashore." Such pillars were dedicated to a god, usually Thor. Ships and pillars then drifted west with the current along the south coast. Ingolf stopped for winter behind a point of land still called Ingolf-shöfdi, a waste of sand and water below the ice field of Vatnajökull. Hjorleif, preferring to rely on his own judgment, continued on southwest for another hundred miles, and rounded the southernmost bend of the coast into a cove (*vik*) west of a stretch of marsh and sand (Myrdalssandr). He built two halls to overwinter, at the site still known as Hjorleifshöfdi. The two parties spent their first winter at opposite ends of the south coast lowland, largely a mass of volcanic sand.

When spring came Hjorleif, disregarding sand and latitude, decided to sow. Having only a single ox he hitched his Irish thralls to the plow. These killed the ox, blamed it on a forest bear (of which there were none), and tricked Hjorleif into scattering his men in pursuit of the supposed bear, thus being able to kill Hjorleif and his Norsemen. The Irishmen took the women, goods, and the ship's boat and fled to rocky islands a few miles to the southwest, still known as Vestmannaeyjar, *vestmann* being the Norse name for Irish. Ingolf's party, resuming the westward search for the pillars, found the body of Hjorleif and the abandoned ship, located the Irishmen and killed them. Their second winter was spent at Hjorleifshöfdi, the third farther west on the Olfus River. At this time the high pillars were found. They had been carried by the westward current alongshore to the end of the south coast and drifted ashore on the west coast. Ingolf, true to his pagan faith, built "his home where his pillars had come ashore, and lived at Reykjavik, and the pillars are there to this day in the living room," said the *Landnamabok*. Ingolf and his men took up homesteads from the Olfus River to Hjalfjord, north of Reykjavik, and were the founding fathers of Iceland. According to the saga, their location was determined by augury of drift of pillar posts, not by inspection of land and harbors.

### LANDNAMA

At that time Harald Fair Hair, beginning with the south of Norway, was bringing the Norse communities under his rule as a unified kingdom. All the land and waters, fresh or salt, were declared property of the king, the people to be tenants by his grace and at his convenience. Nobles and commoners were dispossessed of ancient rights and estates or were given a precarious tenure. To people who had lived by the usages of their own community this was resented tyranny, which would put an end to the viking freedoms of feud and raid. The people of the western fjords, who had known no authority beyond that of their local lords, resisted stoutly and were finally reduced when Harald was able to overcome them by an attack from the sea. Many left with their ships, thanes, thralls, and possessions to find new homes beyond the reach of the king. Iceland was their main refuge, and they went there by whole kindreds with their dependents and whatever they owned. Ari wrote in the *Islendigabok*: "There began a great emigration here out of Norway until King Harald placed a ban upon it because he feared that the country would be abandoned."

At the end of the century the vikings who had settled in Ireland and northern Scotland also were under strong pressure from the resurgent Irish. Many sought a peaceful home in the north, bringing with them Irish thralls, and some Irish wives. Some had become Christians. "Some kept to Christianity to the time of their death, but it was rarely continued in their descendants." Both *Landnamabok* and *Islendigabok* reported that Iceland was fully occupied within sixty years (before 940), so that thereafter there was no more taking of land. The four hundred families recorded in the *Landnamabok* were its elite, the old settlers, vikings once, and many of noble blood. The total immigration amounted to a good many thousands, by far the greatest number of Europeans to remove overseas until well into the sixteenth century.

The *Landnamabok* is register both of the founding families of Iceland and of their seats. It traces their genealogy and intermarriages, the order in which the land was occupied, and to some extent the internal migrations. The book begins with the land taken in the southwest where Ingolf first settled, and follows around the northwest coast and so continues clockwise around the island.

The bay of Breidafjord, in the northwest, where the explorer Floki had found sealing and fishing so attractive that he neglected to prepare for winter, had Thorolf Mostrarskegg as pioneer settler, a great sacrificer and believer in Thor. He too cast into the sea his seat pillars with the likeness of Thor carved on them to have Thor tell him where to build. They were found ashore on a headland about midway of the south shore of the fjord. Thorolf built his seat there and a great temple, which he dedicated to Thor together with all the land he had taken. On Hellgafel (Holy Mountain, the locality still thus known) he ordained a sanctuary where neither man nor beast should be harmed. A hallowed place was set aside also by the seashore where the Thing or assembly was held. Later this was profaned by bloodshed and therefore it was removed up the peninsula "where it is now. It was then a great holy place, and Thor's stone still stands there, on which the men were broken who were sacrificed, and beside it is the ring of judgment where men were sentenced to sacrificial death." Thorolf's son Hallstein settled on the north coast of Breidafjord, offered sacrifice to Thor, and prayed for pillars for his high seat, whereupon a great pine tree drifted ashore that provided pillars for nearly all the homesteads of those parts. Hallstein also went raiding into Scotland and brought back thralls, which he sent to saltworks on islands in the bay. (By what means did they make salt from sea water?)

Aud the Deep-Minded was another progenitor of families on Breidafjord. The Icelandic account elaborates on the Faeroes saga. She had married the viking Olaf the White, who had made himself king of the country about Dublin and then was killed in battle. Aud and her son Thorstein left for the Hebrides, where Thorstein married the daughter of a viking and had a son and six daughters. In association with Sigurd, Earl of Orkney, Thorstein conquered Caithness and Sutherland, Ross and Cromarty, but fell in battle by treachery of the Scots (Irish). Aud, being at that time in Caithness, had a ship built secretly in the forest and sailed to Iceland by way of the Orkneys and Faeroes, marrying off daughters of Thorstein on the way, to found noted lineages. In Iceland she selected wide holdings about Hvammsfjord in the inner part of Breidafjord and distributed land among her followers. Having been baptized a Christian, she set up crosses for her observance of devotions. After her death her kindred built there a stone altar to make their pagan sacrifices.

The *Landnamabok* treats of the occupation of Iceland by its four quarters, each having its district Thing before a general assembly or Althing was established. The north coast quarter "became most densely settled of all Iceland," despite its frontage on a sea subject to ice drift. It had long sheltered fjords flanked by less rugged country than elsewhere, long river courses, and was farthest from the ice caps (*jökulls*) and the lava flows and volcanoes. The quarter of the eastern fjords, with less usable land than that of the north or west, was reported as first to become fully settled. That of the south was least and last; "here storm and surf made landing difficult because of the open and harborless coast." Also it was hemmed inland by ice cap and volcano.

## RESOURCES OF ICELAND

The greater part of Iceland is a waste of ice caps and of vulcanism, lava flows and detritus of unweathered cinders. The soils are acid and humic to excess, of low fertility and likely to be poorly drained and aerated. The growing season, long considering the latitude, is cool, humid, and often cloudy. It was soon found out that high latitude and cool marine climate placed the country beyond the limits of grain growing. It was a land of heath, moor, marsh, and bog. The *Islendigabok* said that at the time of settlement Iceland was covered with woods from mountain to sea, a generous exaggeration of the amount of woody growth. In sheltered valley locations trees such as mountain ash, might grow to greater size than shrubs. For the most part they were dwarf birches and willows. Heaths were and are the most extensive plant association. Lichens (Iceland moss) covered sun-warmed rock faces. On sun-facing, well-drained spots, upland grasses and gaily flowering herbs found a place. In short, the floristic assemblage resembled northern Scandinavia and the northernmost British Isles.

Bird life was varied and abundant along the shores. Waterfowl were a primary resource to the settlers, as were seals. Occasionally whales stranded and were used as food. The fjords gave good fishing by line and net, and the rivers provided salmon, always prized by Germanic peoples. The settlements of the west coast were most richly provided with seals, herring, cod and its kind, capelin, and the flesh and eggs of waterfowl taken in rookeries on islands and headlands. The flightless great auk was hunted, the eider duck

Launching a Boat, from Icelandic *Jonsbok* (Nansen).

protected for its down. Fishing, hunting, and collecting along the coasts were quite as rewarding as in Norway. These were free to all, were followed mostly by the humble folk, and were of casual interest in saga and chronicle.

The coast was important also for collecting driftwood, brought mainly to the south coast by the westward-setting Irminger Current. As shown by the drift of Ingolf's seat pillars, wood was thus carried also around the southwest cape of Reykjanes into bays of the west.

The seeds of a native rye grass, *melur*, growing on heat-storing coastal sands and on volcanic rock, were gathered, ground, and made into bread. A meal was prepared from Iceland moss by tedious processing. Heath and moor yielded the same berries as in Scandinavia.

The sagas say a good deal about horses, occasionally mentioning one by name. The sagas dealt with prestigious people, and horses were marks of prestige and had special care. The landed proprietors lived mainly by animal husbandry; their farmsteads, so called, were in our terms modest stock ranches. The impression given is that in the early years these were chiefly stocked with neat cattle for milk and that sheep became important later. There is slight reference to pigs.

The wild vegetation gave browse of willows and birch. Browsing of heaths was important; here there was also some grazing of interspersed native grasses. Hay was cut in the marshes for winter feed. Continued browsing favored to some extent the reproduction of grasses and herbs over woody growth. Fire was used to clear land, as is suggested by carrying fire about a tract as part of the procedure of establishing title. Gradually the wild vegetation was modified to produce more grass forage.

The homestead consisted of dwelling house and separate structures for the shelter of animals and the storage of fodder. On suitable land nearby an enclosed meadow (*tun*) was established and dressed with manure to provide hay. Beyond were grass plots (*angar*), mainly serving as stock pasture. Farthest removed from the homestead (*gard*) were the high pasture grounds (*affrettir*), where the stock ranged unattended until it was driven in at the onset of winter.[3] Winter was the limiting season on the economy of the gard. Feed often was exhausted before the end of winter, the stock starving.

[3] *Thule*, vol. 23, pp. 15–16.

## ICELANDIC LIFE AND CULTURE

Houses were built of volcanic rock, earth, turf, and thatch. Lacking trees, the settlers imported wood for roof timbers, furniture, tools and boats. Homesteads were established in the interior wherever there was useful land. Along the fjords they were strung along the water's edge. It was a wholly rural population, manorial in rudimentary fashion. Merchant ships came from Norway to visit from fjord to fjord, bringing articles of clothing, hardware, lumber, and corn to trade for hides, wool, and possibly eiderdown. Trade in fish came later, and was organized by Hanse and English merchants. Occasionally an Icelander is mentioned as landholder, ship owner, or merchant at sea. The picture of commerce is most obscure. There were no towns. The old place names have survived in number, especially of the gards, named after founder, physical site, or a remembered event. The places where a Thing was held may be thus identified and also places of sacrifice or sanctuary. Congregation beyond the members of a household was on special and infrequent occasions, not a manner of living.

The Christian influences brought by the Norse from Ireland died out with that generation, perhaps leaving a gentling influence on the erstwhile vikings. Human sacrifices were given up, not so that of horses. When the Althing decided to accept Christianity about 1000 A.D., one of the stipulations was that the people should continue to have the right to sacrifice in the old manner. This was a remarkable concession, since Christianity generally suppressed the sacrifice and eating of horse meat practiced by Germanic peoples.[4]

[4] Horses of larger breed were brought from Norway. Did the Irish Norse introduce the Celtic pony that was distributed from Wales and Ireland to the Hebrides and Shetlands and thus establish the breed of Iceland pony?

Iceland, originally a land of vikings, shortly became the most peaceful country of Europe. It was settled by men who recognized no authority other than their own, which they organized in their new home as a republic, governed by the Althing until the capitulation to Norway in 1262. The vikings who occupied Iceland became homesteaders, stay-at-homes, forsaking their raiding habits at sea. The exceptions are rare and early.

Iceland was a refuge, not another land that promised wealth. Its settlement marks the beginning of the end of the viking period. The greater immigration came because it was an empty and distant land where one might live free of subordination to the Norwegian king. Others came in number from the Celtic fringe of the British Isles, where they were hard pressed by the natives. Iceland and the Faeroes being available as havens. The Faeroes had been stocked with sheep that provided a living for a modest number of land takers. Iceland had room for many more if they were able to wrest a living from a land that offered very small advantage of climate and fertility. "The land was fully occupied in sixty years and thereafter there were no more settlers" (*Landnamabok*).

Shortly Iceland was overpopulated with both people and livestock. Any year of excessive wetness or of deficient warmth brought want and loss. The first year of great famine occurred in 975, forty years after the end of land taking. When Christianity was accepted, one of the conditions was that the old laws should stand as to the exposure of infants (*Islendigabok*).

There is very little mention of exports, and probably there was little. The export of fish products began much later by Hanse and Bristol merchants. Hides were available in surplus, and perhaps wool. The colony depended to a considerable extent on the wealth it had brought. The viking

founders came in their own ships, laden with their possessions from Norway and Ireland, including the loot of raids.
While funds lasted they bought grain for bread and beer,
clothing and shoes, lumber for homes and boats, iron implements. In time the visits of merchant ships fell off. The
people became almost wholly dependent on the subsistence
the island afforded, living mainly in landlocked isolation.
The material decline of Iceland was under way in the eleventh
century and was aggravated by the annexation to Norway.
The former vikings, having become dispersed homsteaders,
remained such without developing a class of artisans and
tradesmen.

As the viking days became memories of a greater past,
they were told in sagas, from generation to generation. Pride
of lineage was thus passed on. Events were carefully retained
in proper location and time. Oral transmission also incor-
porated legends of remote origins. To say truly, what had
been was an obligation that went with the telling. By the
twelfth century scholars began to write down the sagas of
the pagan past, adding only a little Christian editing. Christian Iceland, inward-directed, took greatest interest in the
pagan viking period and produced and preserved an heroic
literature.

# CHAPTER VI GREENLAND AND VINLAND

## NOTICES OF LAND BEYOND ICELAND

Some time after 900 a ship on its way from Norway to Iceland was caught in a storm and driven west until it raised a coast of rocky islands and cliffs, to be known thereafter as Gunnbjörns Skerries. No landing was attempted, and the location is undetermined. Perhaps the sailors sighted some part of the bleak and hazardous east coast of Greenland. A tradition of land to the west spread in Iceland.

The next mention of the skerries is from the latter part of the century. The participants were from west fjord settlements of Iceland. The principal figure, Snaebjorn Gaeti, was a descendant of distinguished vikings who had become rich by loot taken in Ireland and elsewhere in the British Isles. The party set off in search of the Gunnbjörns Skerries and found land, where they overwintered. The indications are that the party landed near the southeast end of Greenland. They built a hall which became snugly buried under snow. When melting began in late winter they dug themselves out and went out to fish and hunt. Accumulated dissensions broke into fighting in which Snaebjorn and others were killed, the rest taking ship for Norway, where they landed in Halogaland, in northernmost Norway, above the Arctic Circle. The survivors later got back to Iceland, where another lot of killings took place.

The account as given in *Landnamabok* was mainly

100

concerned with the homicides, some of which were quite gory, the geographical details being casual. Part of the trouble that broke out at the winter base concerned a purse of money found in a burial mound. A European ship therefore had preceded them to that harbor, perhaps a Norse ship that was lost voyaging to Iceland. Their remarkable return from Greenland to Arctic Norway is mentioned in three words: "They made Halogaland." The victims in each of the three killings are named and the manner of their death is told.

## THE SETTLEMENT OF GREENLAND BY ERIC THE RED

Iceland had been fully appropriated and allotted. The old sea roving had given way to sedentary living on farmsteads. People and livestock had increased to the limit of subsistence and had gone through a great famine (975–976). It was time to find out whether the land to the west was worth settling. In 982 Eric the Red, a lesser and trouble-prone landholder of the western quarter, was exiled for his part in a feud and ordered to stay away long enough for tempers to cool, probably for three years. Perhaps he might find a new land for a fresh start. He and his men would need to subsist for years on what they could procure from strange waters and shores. The hardihood of the enterprise was not in the distance to be covered, which was known not to be great, but in the confidence that they could live for an indefinitely long time off an unknown sea and land.

Eric took his ship west to the barren coast of East Greenland, cliff- and glacier-rimmed, and then turned south "to see whether he would find land to settle" (Saga of Eric the Red). He followed south around the southern tip of Greenland and then turned up the west coast, attractive with fjords as great and green as any in Iceland and of sunnier

101

and warmer summers (map 10). The first winter was spent on an island he called Eirikseye, at the mouth of Eiriksfjord. He had located the best part of Greenland, soon to become known as the Eastern Settlement, now the District of Julian-

Map 10. The Greenland Settlements.

haab. The encampment of the first winter was about ten miles north of Julianehaab.[1] In the spring he went up Eiriksfjord (now Tunugdliarfik) to select the site for his future homestead, and then followed up the west coast, naming places far and wide. A greater reconnaissance to the north was made the following year. The third winter was again spent at Eirikseye. In 985 he came back to Iceland with the news of the new and promising land.

Eric had passed three years exploring the western coast of Greenland, locating what came to be known as the Eastern and Western Settlements and continuing north to about the Arctic Circle. He found the only two tracts where the fjords are rimmed by soil and vegetation sufficient to support animal husbandry. These verdant fringes below the great ice cap gave him the idea to call the country Greenland. The name would recommend it to the landless colonists he hoped to bring, nor was it improper. There would be good pasture and meadow for hundreds of homesteads, excellent fishing and seal hunting in the fjords, and also bird rookeries and driftwood along the outer coast. There was land game, lacking in Iceland. His party had lived well, summer and winter, and returned in full number and good condition. He could invite families in good conscience to leave overcrowded Iceland and follow him to the new country.

In the summer of 986 Eric led a fleet from the western fjords of Iceland, by one account twenty-five, by another thirty-five ships, carrying families, livestock, and household goods. Fourteen ships made it to Greenland; the rest turned back or were lost. The number of pioneer settlers is estimated as four to five hundred. The greater part took up their homesteads in the district Eric had chosen for his own home. It was known thereafter as the Eastern Settlement, although

[1] Jones, Map 3, gives a reconstruction of the topography of the Eastern Settlement by archaeologic location.

103

southern would have been more proper. The rest went on about three hundred miles farther to the northwest to found the Western Settlement, extending to within a hundred miles of the Arctic Circle. It is the present District of Godthaab.[2]

In the Eastern Settlement few homesteads were located along the hundred mile frontage on the open sea. Most were in the interior fjords, forty miles or more back from the headlands. As is commonly true of fjords, the best land was found about the head of the fjord. Eric returned to the site he had chosen, far up the fine fjord he had named after himself, and built there his great hall and homestead, Brattahlid. Here as untitled lord he presided over the affairs of the colony. Gwyn Jones, visiting Eric's fjord and the foundations where Eric's hall had stood, wrote: "It was here that living conditions were easiest. The summer though short was warm and pleasant and it is noticeable that the richest herbage is still to be found on the sites of these old Norse farms. The situation of the Hill Farm at Brattahlid is positively idyllic, with its dark and sparkling stream, its luscious dark green pastures, and the low ramparts of hills which protect it on all sides."[3]

The Western Settlement, lying close under the Arctic Circle, had a shorter growing season and also smaller tracts of land suited for pasture and meadow. It is thought to have held about a fourth of the homesteads, and these were smaller than in the Eastern Settlement. There was better hunting and the advantage of being much nearer to Nordrsetr.

The name Nordrsetr was applied to all the uninhabited coasts north beyond the Western Settlement as far as they

[2] Aage Rousell, *Farms and Churches in the Mediaeval Norse Settlement of Greenland*, vol. 89 of *Meddelelser om Grønland* (Copenhagen, 1941). This is an admirable study of structures, their sites, functions, and contents. "Farms" to the number of 274 were examined.

[3] Jones, pp. 50–51.

were visited by summer hunting parties. Occasionally a party might overwinter there by choice or mishap. Roughly, Nordrsetr lay beyond the Arctic Circle, along the margins of what is now known as Davis Strait and Baffin Bay. Disko Bay and Island, about at Lat. 70° N., were the parts most regularly and successfully entered. Nansen stressed the meeting about Disko of the icy waters moving south from Baffin Bay with the warmer waters drifting north up the Greenland coast. The latter is the last remnant of the warm westward drift across the Northern Atlantic known as the Irminger Current along the south coast of Iceland. It passes about the south end of Greenland and turns north up the west coast carrying driftwood from across the Atlantic as far as Disko Bay.

Nordrsetr was very important to the Greenland settlements. Here they found seals in greatest number. Here they were within the range of a rich and economically valuable Arctic fauna, first of all walrus, but also polar bears, Arctic foxes, caribou, white falcons, and eider ducks. On shore, along the edge of the ice, and inland they had hunting of a yield and diversity unknown in Iceland. Companies assembled each summer to go north by ship and boat for months of hunting. Nordrsetr provided a large supplement to the product of their homesteads. The northern expeditions gave them pelts, ivory, oil, and other things that brought a good price in Europe. And they could look forward each year to adventure and social congregation in camp and on shipboard. Without Nordrsetr life in the settlements would have been a good deal harder and more meager.

Aside from the summer excursion to Nordrsetr life resembled that in Iceland. As had been done in Iceland, the land was cleared by burning, the tracts that could be made to serve as pasture or meadow fewer and smaller than in Iceland. When all suitable land had been appropriated there were about three hundred homesteads, some with only a few acres. The winters, longer and markedly colder than in Iceland, demanded more and better shelters. These were necessary for all animals. Such structures, outlying or attached to the houses, appear in remarkable number on the maps of homesteads in the Roussell monograph.

The Greenland settlements were better provided with building materials than were available in Iceland. Stone and turf were used for walls. In contrast to the lava of Iceland the Greenlanders had fissile rocks available, slabs of gneiss, sandstone, and granite that could be laid in courses and sometimes split by hand. The abundance of driftwood was of great and enduring advantage, for roof timbers and fuel. The Greenlanders did not lack fuel, every homestead having its hot bath. (Roussell did not find one privy.)

> The timber suffers no injury from its long journey. The bark and branches are worn off so that it is ready for immediate use, and there is no question of qualitative deterioration, enclosed by ice as it is for most of the voyage from Siberia across the polar sea. When at last it is thrown ashore, in a cold climate and impregnated with salt, it can last long. And so, when Erik the Red arrived in Greenland's desolate fjords the coast must have been literally congested with wood, building timber and firewood for many years. . . .
>
> It is a remarkable feature that even those sites that are farthest from the shore reveal an almost prodigal use of timber, sometimes in quite unnecessarily robust dimensions.[4]

The Greenlanders led a "relatively peaceful life of sheep farming, hunting, and fishing."[5] Refuse heaps show that cattle, sheep, goats, and dogs were kept and that wild fowl, seal, walrus, polar bear, caribou, hare, and fox were taken, some brought from the north. Fish remains are minor, but fish are known to have been a major food. The diet was fish, flesh, and fowl, and milk products.

[4] Roussell, pp. 23–24.
[5] Michael Wolfe, *American-Scandinavian Review*, vol. 49, pp. 380–387.

Iceland was fully settled in sixty years, as the chronicles stressed. Greenland needed less time. Nansen thought that the population at its maximum may not have exceeded two thousand. Others have placed it higher, some by several thousand. Calculations have been made by number of homesteads, not all of them contemporaneous. The current population of the Julianehaab and Godthaab districts, the modern equivalents of the Eastern and Western Settlements, is around five thousand, mostly Eskimo. In Norse times it is unlikely to have exceeded that number at its maximum and may well have been less. Norse Greenland had perhaps one inhabitant to twenty in Iceland.

The Viking Age passed everywhere before the end of the tenth century as the wild, free life of raiding overseas was lost. In Scandinavia the viking chiefs were brought under control of the kings of nation-states. Many emigrated with their following to distant northern islands, where they became sedentary stockmen and fishers. Eric the Red represented the transition from one way of life to another. Outlawed from Norway by order of the king and from Iceland by the Thing, he found Greenland and became the quiet and capable leader of a community in which peaceful living largely replaced violence and blood feuds. The founders of Iceland were still celebrated in the sagas as having been vikings, but not so the colonizers of Greenland, except Eric.

Eric was one of the last of the old guard, faithful to the Nordic gods and ways. His son Leif is presented as the champion of the new order. The sagas say that, having visited Norway, he was sent back by King Olaf to preach the Christian faith. This, it is said, he did with instant success, his mother being credited with building the first church. However, the Vinland voyage on which he went, and the succeeding ones, have few Christian overtones, suggesting a more gradual conversion. Christianity spread rapidly after

1000. In time there were twelve churches in the Eastern and four in the Western settlement, rather many because of the dispersed living. The church ruins and in particular their graveyards have yielded much of the known record of life.

## VINLAND—THE SOURCES

The earliest notice of Vinland is in the *Gesta* of Adam of Bremen, written about 1070. Adam composed a sort of world geography, much of it from classical authors, parts from observation or what he had been told. He had been for a time with King Svein in Denmark and collected there information and misinformation about the northern seas. Of Iceland he concluded: "They thus lead a holy life in simplicity as they do not strive after more than what nature gives . . . I regard this people as happy, whose poverty none covets." The people of Greenland were like those of Iceland "but more cruel, and trouble sea farers by predatory attacks"; however, they were turning to Christianity. (The remark suggests that his information was out of date and referred to the beginning of the century. I do not know that viking raids were then still being carried on.)

The brief statement on Vinland is: "Moreover he [King Svein] mentioned yet another island which has been discovered by many in that ocean and which is called 'Winland' because vines grow there of themselves and give the noblest wine. And that there is abundance of unsown corn we have obtained certain knowledge not by fabulous supposition, but from trustworthy information of the Danes."[6] By that time Vinland was known in Denmark as a land that had been visited repeatedly, and was notable for its abundance of wild grapes and wild grain, both basic elements also in the sagas.

Most of the lore about Vinland was told in sagas, two

6 The translations of the *Gesta* are by Nansen.

of which, despite their names, are traditions of voyaging to Vinland. They are the Greenlanders' Saga and the Saga of Eric the Red, also known as the Karlsefni Saga. Both are thought to have been written down in the thirteenth century; the existing copies were made a good deal later.[7] They were composed from two different traditions of Vinland voyaging, in part dealing with different personalities and events, and in important parts contradictory and irreconcilable. It is desirable therefore to summarize each separately.

### The Greenlanders' Saga

The Greenlanders' Saga credits the discovery of land beyond Greenland to Bjarni Herjolfsson, in the year 986. He was a merchant shipowner engaged in trading between Iceland and Norway, spending one winter in Norway, the next with his father in southwestern Iceland, where Ingolf had pioneered, whose kinsman Bjarni was. Returning there from Norway in the summer of 986 he found that his father had sold the homestead and gone with Eric to live in Greenland. Bjarni wished to spend the winter with his father and so asked his shipmates whether they would go with him into a sea none had entered. They thus agreed.

After they had sailed west for three days they got into fog (i.e., the cold East Greenland Current) and a north wind which continued for many days, so that they lost all track of their course. When the sun came out they hoisted sail again and after a day sighted land. This land was of low hills and forest-covered, whereby Bjarni knew that it was not Greenland. Leaving the land to port (that is turning north), they sailed on and after two days sighted another land. This second land Bjarni again knew was not Greenland since it lacked glaciers, was flat and covered with woods.

---

[7] Gwyn Jones serves as guide. He has translated both, noting discrepancies in the manuscripts. I have relied on his translation.

The crew wished to land and take on wood and water, but Bjarni ordered them to hoist sail and go out again to sea. For three days they had southwest wind and then came in sight of a third land that was mountainous and had glaciers. Bjarni said that this land looked to be good for nothing, and so they continued along it without lowering sail. They stood out again to sea with a fresh and following (west) wind for four days until they came to the fourth land. Bjarni told the men "this is very like what I am told about Greenland." In the evening they landed under the cape of Herjolfsness, where his father had taken up his homestead and given his name to the cape. Bjarni settled with his father and gave up his voyaging.

The account is matter of fact and acceptable geographically. In early summer a ship sailing west from Iceland might well encounter north wind and great and continuing fog. The men drifted on until they got beyond the fog. When they sighted a forested land of low hills, Bjarni knew that they had gotten into latitudes well below Greenland and so turned about to get to the north, with intermediate sightings of land. The first land seen has been considered to be Newfoundland, the second Labrador, the third Baffin Island. The sight of glaciers on Baffin Island placed them well to the north of the Greenland settlements. It is unlikely that they could have made the final leg of the voyage coming straight to his father's home on the evening of the same day they sighted Greenland, Herjolfsness being farthest south of all homesteads. The story was further embroidered by having Bjarni make his only landing by sailing straight to his father's dooryard, a place he had not seen and the location of which he could not have known.

For the next fourteen years nothing more was done about discovery. The Greenlanders' Saga tells of a trip Bjarni made to Norway in the year 1000, where he told of his travels and was reproached for lack of curiosity that he had learned nothing more of the lands he had sighted. In the same year it is said that "Leif, son of Eric the Red of Brattahlid, went to see Bjarni Herjolfsson, bought his ship from him, and found her a crew." Leif Ericsson took up the quest Bjarni had failed to follow. Leif persuaded his father to take charge of the venture, but as Eric was riding down to board the ship he fell off his horse and was injured, and thus the famous voyage set out from Eiriksfjord under command of Leif.

They sailed out to sea and came first to the land that Bjarni had sighted last before reaching Greenland. They put off a boat and went ashore. Nowhere was grass to be seen. Inland were great glaciers, and the land between glacier and strand was a slab of rock, barren and useless. Leif named it Helluland (flat stone land), after which they returned to the ship.

The second land to which they came was low and covered with woods. There were stretches of white sand wherever they went, shelving gently into the sea. This land Leif named Markland (woodland), after which they hastened back to sea.

Again they went out to sea and were two days before sighting the third land. First they went ashore on an island to north of the mainland. Here they tasted dew on the grass and found it most sweet. They next sailed the ship into a sound between the island and a cape that stood out from the land. They passed west beyond the cape into wide shallows where the ship went aground at low tide, it being a long sight from ship back to sea. They went (by boat) to land where a stream flowed out of a body of water. At flood tide they took the ship into the river and anchored it in a lake. Here they unloaded, built their booths, and decided to spend the winter and build a great hall. River and bay had many salmon, greater than they had ever seen before.

111

They thought the cattle they had brought would need no fodder over winter. Indeed there was no frost, and the grass hardly withered. A statement of the length of day in midwinter has remained uncertain as to meaning except that they found themselves in unaccustomed low latitude.

Having finished building the hall Leif sent out scouting parties, always to return by night. One evening the German Tyrkir, whom Leif called his foster father, came back late in a state of excitement in which he was speaking German. When he had calmed down sufficiently to talk in Norse he told that he had found grapevines and grapes, and assured the others that he knew what he was saying, having been born where such were no rarity. Leif thereafter busied the men at gathering grapes, cutting vines, and felling trees for timber. In spring he sailed home with a full cargo, having named the land Vinland.

So much for the items of geographical bearing in the voyage of Leif, who never returned to the land of his discovery. His father and many others having died of a great sickness during the winter, Leif stayed in Greenland to take care of the affairs at Brattahlid and be the leader of the colony.

The next visit to Vinland was by Leif's brother Thorvald, to whom Leif gave the use of the ship. Nothing was recorded of the voyage until they got to Leifsbudir, as the place where Leif had been was called. They overwintered there quietly, catching fish for their food. In spring Thorvald sent a party west along the coast in the ship's boat to explore in that direction. These spent the summer in a beautiful and well-wooded country, with beaches of white sand between woods and sea. They found numerous islands and shoals, but no human habitations except for one island in the west, where they came upon a granary built of wood. They returned to Leifsbudir that autumn.

The next summer Thorvald took the ship east along the coast and then north. Heavy weather drove the ship ashore on a cape and broke its keel, whereby the cape was called Kjalarnes (keel cape), a locality since in dispute. Farther on they entered the next inlet behind a forested headland, the entire company going ashore. Thorvald thought it a lovely place, where he would like to build his homestead. The first contact with natives took place here. On the beach inside the headland they saw three mounds, which turned out to be three skin boats, with three men sleeping under each. All were killed save one who ran away with one of the boats. Looking farther they spied some humps at a distance which they guessed might be habitations. The Norsemen decided to take a nap, from which they were roused by the approach of a fleet of countless skin boats. The Norse retired to the ship. The Skraelings (natives) shot at them for a while and then disappeared. Thorvald was mortally wounded by an arrow and asked to be buried on the headland where he had wished to live. The ship returned to their comrades (i.e., to Leifsbudir), spent another winter there, gathered grapes and vines, and then went back to Eiriksfjord.

Eric's third son, Thorstein, is next to come into the saga. He took the same ship, his wife Gudrid, and a crew to bring back the body of his brother. They did not make it but were storm-tossed all summer, and at the beginning of winter made land in a fjord of the Western Settlement. Sickness broke out and many died, including Thorstein. Here the saga introduced a tale of how the dead Thorstein rose from his bier to prophesy that Gudrid would marry an Icelander, have many and fine children, and live a long and happy life. The Icelander appeared the next summer in the person of Thorfinn Karlsefni, coming in his merchant ship to Eiriksfjord. With Leif's approval he married the widowed Gudrid and took up the Vinland quest. Gudrid provides the link of continuity that attaches Karlsefni to the Eric household.

Karlsefni and Gudrid made the fourth expedition from Eiriksfjord for Vinland. Its intent was to found a colony. There were sixty men, five women, and an ample assortment of livestock. Leif again gave them the use of Leifsbudir. The voyage was direct and without event. Shortly after their arrival a whale stranded and provided them with plenty of food, along with the abundant fish, game, and grapes they found. The men engaged in cutting and dressing timber, which they piled on rocks to season. The next summer they made their acquaintance with the natives, again called Skraelings. A large party appeared, coming out of the woods with bundles of different pelts, which they exchanged for food that had been prepared of milk. Early in the second winter the natives returned in greater number, and the exchange was repeated. One of the Skraelings tried to steal some Norse weapons. This led to a sharp fight in which a good many natives were killed. Karlsefni decided that the dangers outweighed the attractions of Vinland and returned to Greenland the following spring with his party and a cargo of vines, grapes and furs.

The final Vinland venture is attributed to Freydis, a natural daughter of Eric the Red. Leif again gave her the use of the house he had built in Vinland. To her own ship she added another belonging to two Icelanders who agreed to go along for a half-share of the profits. During the winter at Leif's house in Vinland, Freydis laid a cunning plot to kill the other party, which she carried out cruelly. In spring she returned with a valuable cargo to Eiriksfjord. Leif, informed of her villainy, could not bring himself to punish his sister but foretold that her offspring would come to no good, which proved to be true.

The saga ends with the good life Karlsefni and Gudrid

later lived in Iceland. Leaving Greenland they first sailed to Norway to dispose of the wares. While there the ship was visited by a southerner, a man from Bremen, who admired the figurehead of Karlsefni's ship and bought it for half a mark of gold (four ounces?). It had been carved of *mösurr* wood that had been brought from Vinland.

Such in brief abstract is the account of Vinland as given in the Greenlanders' Saga, which more properly should be called the Vinland Saga. In the manner of sagas it is built around a dominant person and his family and associates, with careful attention to kinship, residence, movement, and succession of events. The first voyage, by Bjarni Herjolfsson, was discovery by accident of weather. His ship was bought by Leif Ericsson to carry on the discovery. Leif reversed the course of Bjarni, went farther than Bjarni had been, and found Vinland, where he built a hall which served all the subsequent expeditions. There were four such, all by the household of Eric, that of Karlsefni by marriage. The voyage of Thorstein Ericsson ended in failure, but the other three reached Vinland. Leif may have started in the year 1000, and the voyages continued for a decade or so. The saga is told in moving simplicity, spare and clear as to persons, places, and events, with little insertion of anything eerie or supernatural.

*The Saga of Eric the Red/Thorfinn Karlsefni*

The briefer Saga of Eric the Red is also, and more appropriately, known as the Saga of Thorfinn Karlsefni. It does not mention a voyage of Bjarni, gives only a few lines to that of Leif, and says nothing of a separate voyage by Thorvald. Thorstein Ericsson is reported as having set out on a voyage subsequent to Leif's in which the party drifted about the sea for a long time, came in sight of Iceland, saw birds from Iceland, and got back to Eiriksfjord battered and worn.

Eric's fall from his horse, which kept him from taking part, is here associated with the start of Thorstein's voyage. The greater part of the story about Thorstein concerns his brief resurrection to advise his wife Gudrid, about as in the other saga.

Mainly the saga is about Thorfinn Karlsefni and his voyage, in which it has Thorvald take part and also Freydis, Thorvald being killed, shot by a uniped. Three voyages in the Greenlanders' Saga appear here as one. Leif's voyage is presented as the accidental result of a storm-tossed return from Norway by which he came to lands the existence of which he had not dreamed of. Leif found self-sown wheat fields and grapevines. "There were also trees called *mösurr*, and of all these samples were taken, some trees large enough to serve for house building." This is the entire account of Leif's discovery. The name Vinland is not mentioned until Karlsefni enters into the saga.

Karlsefni took the roundabout way from Eastern to Western Settlement, then northwest across Davis Strait and so to the American coast, discovering and naming Helluland and Markland on the way. Farther on they came upon the keel of a ship and therefore named the place Kjalarnes. (By this account Thorvald was alive, had nothing to do with the name, nor was it the place of his death or burial.) The long beaches they sailed by gave rise to the name Furdustrandir, marvel strands. A wild Scots couple was put ashore to run inland and spy out its quality to the south. They returned after three days bringing grapes and self-sown wheat. (They were still a long way to the north.) Next they came to a fjord off the mouth of which was an island they named Straumsey (bird island), there being so many birds that one could hardly set foot between the eggs. (Nansen commented that birds did not nest at that season.) They held on into the fjord, Straumfjord, to pass the winter there. There were mountains and the prospect around was beautiful, but the winter proved hard.

The next spring the further course of the expedition was discussed as to how to find Vinland. One party looked for it turning north by way of Furdustrandir and Kjalarnes. These met with a storm and were shipwrecked off Ireland. Karlsefni sailed south with the main party, continuing for a long time until they came to a river that flowed through a lake into the sea. The sand bars were so large that the river could be entered only at full flood. The place was named Hop (landlocked bay), and here they established themselves and their cattle. Fields of self-sown wheat were on the low ground, and grapevines grew on the hills. They dug trenches in the estuary and caught halibut in them when the tide was out. The streams were full of fish and the forest of game.

Here for the first time the tale resembles the Greenlanders' Saga. Hop is much like Leifsbudir in location, climate, and events. No snow fell in the winter, and the stock continued to graze in the open. Natives, coming in a multitude of skin boats out of the south, offered furs for pieces of red cloth. Three weeks later they reappeared, yelling and waving staves, and chased the Norsemen to a stand among the rocks. The day was saved by Freydis, who stropped a sword on her breasts and put the Skraelings to flight. After more fantastic details Karlsefni decided to abandon the land, though it was well suited for settlement, and returned north to Straumfjord, and then to Greenland. The latter part of the saga is most confused and admits that there were differing accounts of happenings. Also the surviving manuscripts are in disagreement.

Both sagas were written down more than two hundred years after the events. The Greenlanders' Saga has continuity, clarity, and for the most part credible description. It reads well, keeping to the main theme of the Ericsson family.

The other saga puts Karlsefni into the central position, is less well ordered in its telling, and has more extraneous legends introduced. The merits of the two sagas have been differently assessed by different scholars.

## IN NORTHERN MISTS

The Norse voyages to America have had long and formidable study, with little trend to agreement. Serious students have placed Vinland anywhere from the Strait of Belle Isle to Long Island Sound, and even to Chesapeake Bay. Uncritical ones have located it as far afield as Hudson Bay and Florida. The difficulties are numerous and lie in the contradictions between the two sagas as well as in the vagueness of their geography. There is general acceptance of Helluland as Baffin Island, of Markland as lying south of Helluland, and of Vinland as south of Markland. Markland is considered by some as southern Labrador, by others as Newfoundland.

In the Greenlanders' Saga three lands are sighted by Bjarni, from south to north, recognizably described, but not named. Leif gets this information from Bjarni and, backtracking on Bjarni's course, names the three lands. On his return from Vinland Leif takes the direct course home north across the sea. The subsequent voyages to Vinland are direct, between Eiriksfjord in Greenland and the place in Vinland where Leif had built his camp, Leifsbudir. This is straightforward and makes sense. Leif having found Vinland by the roundabout way south along the coast, thereafter it was convenient to take the short north-south route across the sea. This would also have the advantage of avoiding fogs.

Eric's (or Karlsefni's) Saga, which reduces the role of Leif, makes Leif the accidental discoverer of Vinland. According to it Leif leaves to go to Norway, is storm-driven to the Hebrides, where a romantic episode is told at length.

Thence he journeys to the court in Norway, where the king gives him the mission to Christianize Greenland. On the way home he is again storm-driven, this time to lands the existence of which he had not dreamed, very briefly mentioned as to self-sown wheat, grapevines, and *mösurr* wood. Some years later Karlsefni comes to spend the winter at Brattahlid, the saga giving major attention to his wooing of the widowed Gudrid. He then decides to go to find Vinland as the result of what he heard from Leif. Instead of taking the direct course Karlsefni, with ships carrying a hundred and sixty men, livestock, and household goods and going with the intention to colonize Vinland, takes the roundabout and tedious course of sailing three hundred miles north to the Western Settlement, then crossing Davis Strait to Baffin Land, which he is credited with naming Helluland, and then to Markland, the name also credited to him.

This saga transfers to Karlsefni the discoveries of Bjarni and partly those of Leif as told in the Greenlanders' Saga. The ships get to a fjord and island of birds (Straumfjord and Straumsey), where they spend the first hard winter. In the spring the main party goes south to look for Vinland, while a small party turns its search to the north. A number of strange incidents occur which Nansen thought were ancient legends that were woven into the tale.

The Eric/Karlsefni Saga has been of particular interest to those who have tried to chart the route to Vinland. It has notes on distances and some on direction between Helluland and Straumfjord. These and the latter fjord with its fronting island have been construed as the Strait of Belle Isle between Labrador and Newfoundland. In this saga Straumfjord is the key locality, and thereby Vinland has been located in northern Newfoundland. Its data on the course of Karlsefni's sailing are scant, discontinuous, and ambiguous. Nansen thought the repetition of numbers sug-

119

gestive of ritual. To the south of Straumfjord the saga is illegible as to geography, the Hop locality having some resemblance to Leifsbudir, the key site of the Greenlanders' Saga.

The two sagas do not jibe as to voyages or localities. That of the Greenlanders in my opinion is the more credible as to sensible course and sequence of voyages and as to matter-of-fact description of event and place.

Where Vinland lay has raised questions as to what the shoreline and climate were like at that time. Inferences have been made that the coast a thousand years ago was not in its present position. It is known that the melting of the Pleistocene ice caps caused a general rise of sea level, offset in northeastern North America by an upwarping of the land as it was freed of the weight of the ice mass. This elevation of the land is considered as diminishing southward from Labrador to New England, Long Island Sound being the "hinge line" of no crustal change. The warping continued into recent time and may not yet have come to its end. Very little is known of the change of shoreline since the Norse days. The late discovery by Helge Ingstad of a village at the northern tip of Newfoundland which he attributes to the Norse and which has been dated at a thousand years old is approximately at the present shore line (see pp. 182–184 below).

Change of climate since Norse time has also been inferred, in particular by those who have thought to find a northerly location for Vinland. This important and controversial question will serve to lead to a consideration of the vegetation that was found and gave name to Vinland.

## THE CLIMATE OF VINLAND

Vinland was remembered in the sagas for the mildness of its climate and the luxuriant and diverse vegetation, both sagas agreeing. Cattle needed no shelter in winter, and they could find feed at all seasons. Vinland had abundant grass, great trees, and many grapevines. As its story was told and grew by telling in the northern homelands, no snow fell in Vinland.

The name Vinland has bothered those who think of it as in a northern location, such as Newfoundland. One solution was to replace grapes with berries, such as grow in variety in northern countries. This fails to show why Norsemen should have used a strange name for fruits with which they were most familiar. Another proposal was made some eighty years ago that *vin* in this case was not the word for wine or grapes but that it was an old Norse word for pasture. This was answered, Nansen concurring, by showing that the word had passed out of use before Vinland time and was not used as a place name in Iceland or Greenland. The interpretation, however, keeps appearing, most recently with Helge Ingstad's ancient village on the Strait of Belle Isle. (Ingstad admits Vinland as extending south from there.) These alternative explanations of Vinland start from the premise that the country was in the latitudes of Newfoundland and therefore that the name applied to vegetation indigenous there.

Another way out of the northern dilemma has been by postulating a change of climate. There is evidence, discovered in Scandinavia and northern Britain, that the climate of northern Europe was milder in the tenth and eleventh centuries, became more extreme in the thirteenth, and ameliorated in or after the fifteenth. Similar variation has been adduced for Greenland, to be considered later. It has been thus inferred that there were swings of temperature of centennial amplitudes extending across the higher latitudes of the North Atlantic. The changes inferred differ in degree and kind according to the investigator and include duration and areal extent. The climates of the Middle Ages are still a highly speculative matter, even for northern Europe, where they have been most closely studied. Their expression in vegetation is more so.

By transferring modest and meager climatic data from northern Europe across the Atlantic a sufficient change in climate has been construed to postulate a Vinland, a land of grapevines, far to the north of present possibility. The thesis that grapevines grew much farther north at the time of the Vinland voyages is in current vogue. It is strongly advocated by Gwyn Jones, who has written "we can believe in the grapes." In support he notes that Cartier (in 1535) found abundance of grapevines on both sides of the St. Lawrence River. "It may therefore be assumed that in far more favorable climatic conditions, such as obtained at the time of the Vinland voyages, the northern limit of the wild grape included Newfoundland's northern peninsula." He then hedges by adding that perhaps grapes were not met with in that northern tip but were found somewhat farther south.[8]

When Jacques Cartier went up the St. Lawrence River he noted that the woods were matted with grapevines. Although the extensive hardwoods have been removed and with them the mat of grapevines, hardwood trees and grapevines still grow where Cartier saw them. Abbé Provencher in his *Flore Canadienne* of 1862 placed the northern limit of wild grapes at Ile-aux-Coudres, fifty miles below Quebec, which is approximately where Cartier first noted them. They are listed in current floras as native to the St. Lawrence Valley. This most boreal New World extension of wild grapes is still where it was in the time of Cartier. There has been no retreat since then and there is no known basis for inferring one in the five hundred years preceding him.

[8] Jones, p. 86.

The presence or absence of wild grapes is wrongly presented in terms of winter or other temperatures. As climbing vines they depend on supporting trees, and to climb the trees they need sunlight. This they lack in the evergreen coniferous forests but find in deciduous woods. Their ecologic niche requires hardwoods and at least moderately fertile soil and good drainage. The St. Lawrence Valley, of rigorous northern winters, is a land of deep and fertile glacial and water-laid deposits on which grew a deciduous forest of oak, maple, beech, and basswood, bare of leaves for half the year and transmitting partial sunlight during most of the rest. This is the association to which the eastern *Vitis* belongs. It existed also on the Atlantic coast but farther south.

## THE VEGETATION OF VINLAND

The attempts to make Vinland mean something else than a land of wild grapes are refuted by every account. It was thus known in Denmark and Hamburg at a time when men may still have been living who had been to Vinland. And thus early it had the fiction added that it produced most excellent wine. As Eric had named Greenland for its verdant fjords, Leif named the southern land for grapevines unknown to his northern home, as proof that a land of genial clime had been found. As the tale of Vinland was told and retold, the returning ships were imagined as loaded with cargoes of grapes and vines.

The major wild grape of the northeastern Atlantic states is the fox grape (*Vitis Labrusca*), ecologically belonging to the mesophytic deciduous woodlands east of the Appalachians, largely oak, maple, and elm. These woods extend north through southern New England, giving way northward to conifers, the dense and year-round shade of which excludes such vines. A land abounding in such grapevines would thus have been first encountered in southern

123

New England. When Karlsefni came to the landlocked bay of Hop, according to his saga, there were grapevines in all the hilly country, which would fit the moraines of southern New England and their cover of hardwoods.

The location of Vinland might be placed somewhat farther north if a second and lesser species, *Vitis riparia*, is concerned. As its name implies it is found along streams where the waterside provides the needed sunlight. Its northern limit is given as New Brunswick. In size, flavor, and yield of fruit it is inferior to the *Labrusca* grape. The latter was an Indian food of some importance throughout its range. When American colonists came, they soon planted cuttings of selected *Labrusca* kinds, from which our horticultural varieties of the northeastern states are derived. The enthusiasm of the Norsemen would seem to apply to the superior *Labrusca* grape, widely present in the deciduous woodlands and, according to the sagas, of upland habit.

The cargoes of grapes taken back to Greenland were supplied by the imagination of the sagas. Dried samples might be taken, most readily from the lesser *riparia* species, known as frost grape because the fruits hang on the vine into cold weather. The cutting and loading of vines is a little more probable. They are lianas, strong, long, and flexible, a natural cordage that would have been useful in the ways lianas are used in the tropics. These great vines, climbing into the treetops, strong as hawsers, supple as ropes, might have been worth taking back.

Trees were felled in Vinland to be dressed and seasoned as lumber, without mention of their kind. There is no mention of taking masts or spars, in contrast to the later Cabot and Corte Real voyages to Canadian coniferous shores. The Greenlanders perhaps had enough timber of conifers among the driftwood piled on their home shores. Hardwood they lacked, and this was in good supply in southern New England. Both sagas refer to *mösurr* wood. The Karlsefni Saga in its scant notice of Leif says that he took back samples of this wood along with grapes and self-sown grain. In the Greenlanders' Saga Karlsefni took back a block of this wood, which he had carved into a ship's figurehead in Norway, where it was bought at a very high price by a man from Bremen.

*Mösurr* is an old Germanic word, meaning spotted. It survives in English as *measles*, in German as *Masern*, the disease that breaks out in spots. In Medieval English *mazer* was applied to small excrescences on wood, then to such wood. This abnormality, which we call "bird's-eye," occurs in some maples and birches. The interlocking whorls of fibers produce a tough wood and one that takes a high polish. Mazer cups and bowls came to be prized in Europe as attractive and rare. In New England the sugar maple (*Acer saccharum*) frequently takes this aberrant form of growth. Bird's-eye maple, available here in larger dimensions and more commonly than in Europe, became a favorite wood of New England cabinet and gunstock makers in colonial time. Leif was first to recognize the superior New World wood. Karlsefni took a block cut from a large tree to Europe, large enough to be carved into a ship's figurehead, and valued there as a great rarity.

Self-sown grain was mentioned. Nansen was inclined to dismiss it as an ancient and recurrent element in legends of the fortunate islands. Lyme grass provided a self-sown grain to the settlers in Iceland, especially on the broad *sandurs* of its south coast. As the Vinland farers moved along sandy coasts in summer they may have seen tracts of grass with nodding heads that gave the appearance of a grainfield. Or they may have found grassy openings in the woodlands such as the English settlers encountered later, perhaps cleared by fire. There is nothing distinctive about

125

the mention of cereal grass and nothing inappropriate to southern New England. Abundant grapevines and large sugar maples, however, were proper to those parts and not farther north.

## THE SKRAELINGS OF THE VINLAND VOYAGES

The sagas called the natives Skraelings, as did later Norse accounts. In later times the Greenlanders were in contact with Eskimos, always referred to as Skraelings. Thus the thirteenth-century *Historia Norvegiae*: "On the other side of the Greenlanders to the northwest hunters have met with a dwarf people, whom they call Skraelings." The reference is to Greenlanders meeting Eskimos in Davis Strait, perhaps on Baffin Island. Skraeling had the meaning of dwarf and weak physique and perhaps, as Nansen thought, a supernatural quality as of gnome, kobold, or troll. When Norsemen came to know the undersized Eskimo the belittling name was appropriate.

How the name Skraeling came to be applied to the natives of Vinland is unexplained. The *Islendigabok*, written before 1133, tells how, when Eric explored Greenland, there were found habitations and other remains of prior occupants from which it could be seen that the people who had passed that way were like those of Vinland, "whom the Greenlanders call Skraelings." At that time there were no Eskimos living in or near either Greenland settlement. Summer expeditions to Nordrsetr perhaps met with Eskimos well up in Baffin Bay. Such contacts, however, are of later record. The troublesome *Islendigabok* passage may have taken the name Skraeling from an unrecorded meeting to the north with dwarf people and applied it thoughtlessly to Vinland. Or it may have been an interpolation by a later copyist, the original being lost. Both Vinland sagas, known by late versions, call the natives Skraelings. Students who have given Vinland a northern location accept them as Eskimos.

Since Vinland was the first place where Norsemen met natives overseas, their appearance should have had notice. In the Karlsefni Saga the meeting at the southern locality of Hop is thus described: "They were small people, cunning of mien and with bristly hair on their heads. They had big eyes and broad cheeks." However, in the *Hauksbok* version of the saga, "small" is replaced by "dark." The meeting took place where grapevines grew over all the hills. In the Greenlanders' Saga, perhaps at the same meeting, the leader of the natives is noted as a large and comely man. This is all the sagas say of physical appearance except for the uniped of Karlsefni's Saga who shot Thorvald with an arrow and hopped out of sight.

There is no mention of natives in either saga for Leif's voyage of discovery. In the Greenlanders' Saga Thorvald led the second voyage, spent two winters at Leif's old camp, and had his first and fatal meeting with natives the following summer. Karlsefni likewise met no natives until the second summer when a numerous lot came out of the forest, that is, from inland. The natives neither lived on the coast nor were they seen on it, except when traveling by canoe. Vinland therefore was not a land of Eskimos, who made their living by hunting seals, taking seafowl and their eggs, and fishing, and built their villages at places along the sea.

The native boats, reported as skin-covered, have been taken to be Eskimo kayaks or even umiaks. The evidence is rather that they were canoes, such as the northern Algonquian tribes used. Gathorne-Hardy made such objection concerning the nine men Thorvald found sleeping under three beached boats. A kayak is a one-man boat, very rarely built for two. The covered kayak is unsuited to shelter a single sleeper. Gathorne-Hardy cited Jacques Cartier for the St. Lawrence on the Indian habit of sleeping under their overturned canoes when traveling, as these nine were. The episode is out of character for Eskimos.

# NORTHERN MISTS

Perhaps the boats were birchbark canoes, the whitish color and seams suggesting a skin cover to the northmen, who had little opportunity to inspect them. Perhaps a skin cover was used instead of or prior to birch bark. There is no archaeologic evidence. Historically the birchbark canoe was the water craft, admirably light and fast, that served Algonquian tribes wherever they had access to the proper materials.

In both sagas natives appeared in flotillas. In the Greenlanders' Saga the killing of the eight natives by Thorvald is followed by the appearance of a countless fleet of skin boats coming to attack, shooting arrows. In the Karlsefni Saga the Norsemen were first visited at Hop, of southern location, by nine skin boats (in another version a great multitude), coming peaceably. Later a great number of boats came up from the south "like a streaming current," swinging staves in unison and yelling as they attacked. The scene is proper for an Algonquian war party, not for Eskimos or Beothuks.

When the natives first came out of the forest to visit at Leifsbudir they brought packs of furs, "gray furs" (beaver?), sables (marten?), and pelts of other kinds, perhaps as offer of friendship rather than for trading purposes as the Norse thought. The bales of different furs again point to hunting, trapping, and fur-dressing skills such as later made Algonquians the support of the French colony.

Norse reconnaissance was limited to the coast and to short distances inland, and did not come upon any native village. Thorvald's party saw from a distance a number of mounds which they surmised might be habitations. The only structure found was by the boat party Thorvald sent west from Leifsbudir. On an island at the west of their reconnaissance they reported a granary made of wood, *kornhjälm af tre*, literally a grain helmet made of wood, a dome-shaped structure. The eastern Algonquians built round houses in the shape of a cupola or beehive. The frame was of poles bent together and lashed at the top, the covering of bark, such as elm or chestnut. What the Norse found may have been an unoccupied house in which corn had been stored. None of the things told of the people of Vinland applies to Eskimo traits. All of them fit the Algonquian Indians. When North America began to be settled by the French and English, Algonquian tribes held a vast territory, extending from Nova Scotia west across the Great Lakes to the Canadian prairies and south through New England and Pennsylvania into Virginia. All were skilled hunters, trappers, and fresh as well as tidewater fishers. Where the environment permitted they were also agriculturists, living in permanent villages. They met the first white men with friendship and generosity but resisted aggression bravely, as happened later in New England with the Pequots and in King Philip's War. Vinland was first to witness such hostile reaction.

What the sagas say about Skraelings in Vinland fits the historical data on the Indians of New England, all of whom belonged to Algonquian tribes. Vinland, it may be inferred, was occupied by natives ancestral to those later known in New England and the Maritime Provinces of Canada. There is a gap of six hundred years between the Vinland Skraelings and the Massachusetts, Pequots, Mohicans, and other Algonquian tribes of colonial New England. There is no evidence that Algonquian tribes were latecomers to the Atlantic coast, except north of the Gulf of St. Lawrence, where the Montagnais pushed into Labrador and displaced Eskimos. South of this gulf all the people were Indian, Algonquian and Beothuk, the latter the only other ethnic group historically known in the northeast of North America. This primitive and inoffensive Indian people historically occupied Newfoundland. The Vinland Skraelings were neither Eskimo nor Beothuk, with one possible exception.

Skraelings who were Beothuk may have been noticed

129

in the latter part of the Karlsefni Saga. Karlsefni, having left Vinland with a south wind to return to Greenland, landed in Markland. Here they found five Skraelings, one a grown man with a beard, two women, and two boys. They captured the boys, but the others got away and "sank into the ground." The boys were kept and taught to speak Norse. They told their new masters that they had no houses, the people sleeping in caves or holes in the ground. If this is not an extraneous myth, as Nansen thought, but an experience given in the fanciful manner of that saga, it relates to Markland, north of Vinland, occupied by a people different from those of Vinland. Markland is held by some students to be Newfoundland, on better grounds I think than relating it to Labrador as others have done. The Corte Real voyage of 1501 brought back a cargo of captives from Newfoundland, also described as shy and as living in caverns. If the saga is factual as to this episode, it is the first notice of Beothuk Indians.

Three native cultures and peoples occupied the coastal parts of northeastern North America (map 11). The Eskimos were at the north and first became known to the Norsemen beyond the Arctic Circle through expeditions to Nordrsetr, mostly after the eleventh century. There is no evidence of contact with them in the Vinland sagas. Eskimo archaeologic sites extend south through Labrador and across the Strait of Belle Isle into the coasts of the northern peninsula of Newfoundland. By French and English times the Eskimos no longer lived south of Belle Isle. It has been thought that they abandoned their southern range because of the advance of the Montagnais Indians across southern Labrador. A people as strange as Eskimos were to Europeans should have been properly noticed, as indeed they were later.

Most if not all of Newfoundland belonged to the Beothuk. The scant information tells very little of habits or habitation. Primitive and isolated, they were aboriginal people

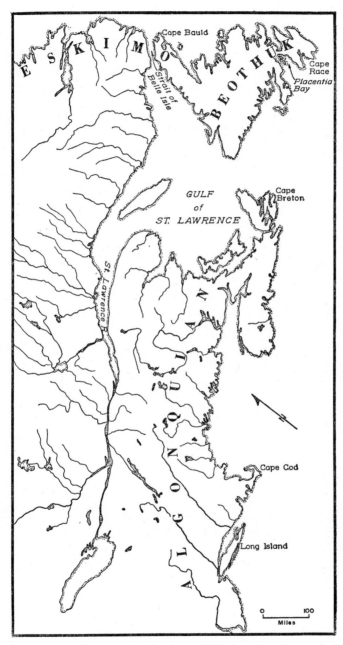

Map 11. Inferred Distribution of Native Peoples at the
Time of Vinland.

131

who withdrew into the last refuge available, which was Newfoundland. A single incident in the Karlsefni Saga may relate to them, given as happening in Markland when Karlsefni returned north from Vinland and is the sole reference to contact with people in Markland. The Beothuks were not the natives who gave trouble to the Norse.

The Vinland Skraelings are recognizable as Indians of the Eastern woodlands, warlike enough to cause abandonment of Norse plans to colonize there. It is concluded that they were an Algonquian people.

## THE LOCATION OF VINLAND

From comment in the Greenlanders' Saga as to the position of the sun on the shortest day, one student placed Vinland in 49° N., another south of Chesapeake Bay.[9]

Attempts to locate Vinland have been made in number, especially by reconstructing the voyage from Karlsefni's Saga. Those who have relied on it mostly have wound up with the Strait of Belle Isle as Vinland, or as its beginnings. By the Greenlanders' Saga Leif backtracked the discovery of Bjarni, going by way of Helluland, Markland, and so to Vinland, without notation of distances. Thereafter the voyages as given by this saga are direct between Greenland and Vinland, without any sailing details. The Karlsefni Saga gives data on days of sail, though these are not continuous, and adds occasional brief and vague topographic notes of headland, inlet, and sandy beach. These uncertain items have been variously assembled into charts purporting to show the sailing route.

The two sagas disagree from the start. Saying nothing of Bjarni's sightings of western lands, the Karlsefni Saga, though agreeing that Leif had been to Vinland ahead of

[9] Jones, pp. 86–87; also E. V. Gordon, *Introduction to Old Norse* (London, 1927), p. 191.

Karlsefni, had Karlsefni make the roundabout and tedious approach by way of Baffin Island which Leif's return from Vinland made unnecessary and senseless. Objection has been made to the Greenlanders' Saga that it is overly simple and clear in having all the voyages go to the same place in Vinland and that it omits mention of Straumfjord. However, if Leif made the coastal reconnaissance from north to south by information from Bjarni and returned by direct route to the family seat at Brattahlid, the later voyages would properly have taken the direct course to the same base in Vinland. That Greenland's dominant family should have continued to conduct the voyages is reasonable, as is their use of the good camp Leif had built in Vinland.

The Erik/Karlsefni Saga, aside from its bias, fantastic episodes, and romantic wooings, raises misgivings. It rather overdoes the matter of being storm-tossed. Leif, starting for Norway, loses his way and gets to the Hebrides. When he later sets out for home from Norway, he gets blown off course again, and makes an accidental landing in a land he had never dreamed of, which was Vinland. Thorstein gets storm-tossed off Iceland and so to Ireland. Straumfjord, its key locality, identified by some with the Strait of Belle Isle, lay to the south of the country (Labrador?) where the eerie Scots couple found and brought back grapes and self-sown wheat. On the island off its mouth (Belle Isle) the birds were so numerous that one could hardly set foot between the eggs, and this, Nansen said, in fall when there were no eggs. One can understand how Nansen was so bemused by contradictory and fabulous elements that he gave up trying to locate Vinland. The Strait of Belle Island as the Norse base in Vinland has most recently been supported by Helge Ingstad's discovery there of a thousand-year-old European village, of which more later.

A
(MAP)
OF
(VINLAND)
from accounts contained in
Old Northern M.SS.
by
CHARLES C. RAFN.

● Inscription-Rock.

MIDDLESEX Cambridge

BOSTON

NORFOLK

MASSACHUSETTS

BAY

BOSTON BAY

ESSEX

PLYMOUTH

KJALARNES

CAPE COD

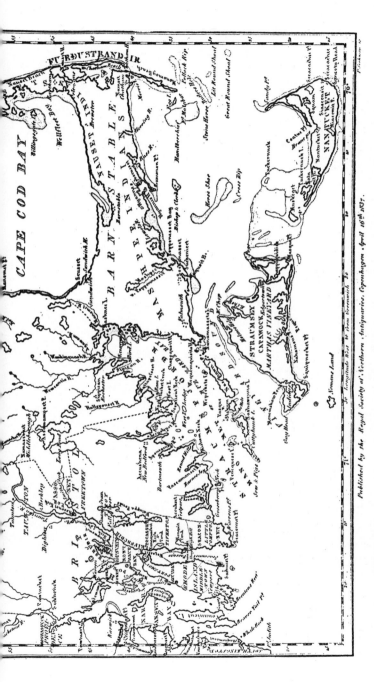

Map 12. Rafn's Reconstruction of Vinland (Supplement to the *Antiquitates Americanae*, Copenhagen, 1841).

Carl Christian Rafn first assembled the documents and proposed in 1834 that Vinland was Rhode Island (map 12). Late in life William Cullen Bryant wrote his meritorious and largely forgotten *Popular History of the United States* (1876). Knowing southern New England well, he liked Rafn's placing of Vinland and thought that Buzzards Bay satisfied best the situation described in the sagas. John Fiske in 1892 favored Massachusetts Bay. Geoffrey Gathorne-Hardy in 1921 made a case for Long Island Sound.[10] All are reasonable choices.

A location in southern New England is in accord with the name, a land of many vines, bearing superior grapes, thus placing it in a deciduous woodland, which here would include well-grown hard maples, some the prized mösurr. There was good pasturage for cattle, which suggests open woods and grassy tracts such as were common in southern New England, and in part were due to Indian burning. The winters seemed most mild to the northmen and in the retelling became more benign. Contacts with the natives, scant as they were, are in agreement with the nature of the Algonquians of New England, in contrast to that of Eskimos. One incident that occurred in Markland (Newfoundland) perhaps is referable to the Beothuks.

The topography of the Greenlanders' Saga agrees with the south of New England. Leif, nearing the place where he was to build his booths, sailed west around a cape into a stretch of shoals. Here the ship went aground, to be refloated at high tide. They took the ship's boat into the mouth of a river where they anchored to overwinter. It was here that Leif built his camp, Leifsbudir, that was to serve the later expeditions. In the next voyage Thorvald sent a boat party on a long reconnaissance west from Leifsbudir, finding many

<hr />

[10] Geoffrey Gathorne-Hardy, *The Norse Discoverers of America* (London, 1921), pp. 271–274.

beaches, islands, and shoals, and at the farthest west an island with a wooden granary. Long Island Sound with its numerous morainic islands, tidal flats, shoals, and beaches fits the conditions. Leifsbudir thus might have been located in Buzzards Bay or somewhere to the west, perhaps as far west as New London.

In the Karlsefni Saga, the Norse followed the coast south for a long time until they came to Hop, a landlocked bay at the mouth of which were so many sandbanks that its river could be entered only at high tide. The resemblance to Leifsbudir has been often remarked. They dug trenches in the tide flats, and when the tide went out they took halibut in them. Gathorne-Hardy cited a parallel from the earliest geography of New England, *The New English Canaan*: "There are excellent plaice and easily taken. They (at flowing water) do almost come ashore, so that one may step but half a foot deep, and prick them up on the sands."

Southern New England, and preferably Long Island Sound, is indicated as the location of Vinland. There is no need of climatic change.

## THE ABANDONMENT OF VINLAND

The voyages to Vinland continued at most for a dozen years; according to some reckonings, for only six. After more than a hundred years there is reference once more to Vinland, a Bishop Eirik of Greenland being recorded in the Icelandic Annals as having gone in 1121 in search of Vinland. Who he was, why he went, and what became of him is not stated. Markland appears again in the Annals for 1347, when a small, rudely built Greenland ship which had been to Markland was storm-driven into a harbor in western Iceland. That is the last Norse word about American shores.

According to the sagas, each party that reached Vinland overwintered at least once; Thorvald reputedly spent three winters there. With the exception of Karlsefni's first winter at Straumfjord, mentioned only in his saga, there was no lack of food. They lived off the land and waters in ease and comfort at all seasons and, unlike their life in Greenland, they did not experience sickness. Karlsefni came to settle, bringing livestock and families, sixty persons by the Greenlanders' version, a hundred and sixty by the other saga.

The Vinland venture was begun and supported by Leif Ericsson. Leif, taking over the affairs at Brattahlid on his father's death, did not return to Vinland. He aided other members of the family to do so, and thus lost two brothers and saw a sister bring shame to the family. Karlsefni, merchant of Iceland, was linked by marriage, undertook to colonize Vinland, and abandoned the enterprise after conflict with the natives.

The sons of vikings had become husbandmen, still inclined to quarrel among themselves but no longer looking forward to raid and combat abroad. For a hundred years and more they had been occupying empty places, first in Iceland and then in Greenland, to raise cattle and sheep. This new land was the best they had found, but it was also the most remote and it would need to be taken from natives who had been hostile. There is no word that anyone thought of tilling the soil, a way of life none knew in Greenland or Iceland. If one had to guard one's home and stock against savages, what was the advantage or profit in staying? They might have foreseen a profitable trade in furs, as the French did later by treating the natives as friends, but instead they attacked the Indians, nor did they have the bent of traders. If they wished to live as they had done in Greenland, inattentive to other prospects of the new country, they did better to go back to their settlements and the familiar hunting of Nordrsetr, and this they did.

That the Norse left evidence of their presence in Vinland is unknown and unlikely. Their contact with natives was slight and brief, too much so to give probability of cultural transfer. Nansen thought the Indian game of lacrosse might have been taken from an Icelandic ball game. Norse words have been claimed to occur in Algonquian language; such exercise in imaginary etymology extended even to a volume on a supposed Norse-Algonquian language. The various claims of Norse buildings that have been advanced from Rhode Island to northern New England cannot be attributed to the temporary encampments of the Vinland voyagers. If there are vestiges they will be found in lesser items, burials, metal weapons or tools, or a rune stone, all such claims offered thus far being unaccepted.

# CHAPTER VII FAILURE OF THE GREENLAND SETTLEMENTS

## THE NARROW LIMITS

The obverse of the question why the Norse colony of Greenland failed is how it survived for five hundred years. Iceland was wholly settled in sixty years, experienced a famine forty years later, and after ten more years Eric took a train of emigrants to Greenland. Fourteen shiploads, we are told, made the crossing, perhaps of the order of five hundred persons. Others came from time to time. Whether Nansen's estimate of a maximum population of two thousand is kept or is doubled or even tripled it did not take long to occupy all the habitable land in Greenland. Karlsefni's expedition to Vinland was in search of additional space, and this was only twenty years after Eric had brought the pioneer settlers to Greenland.

The geography of the Greenland settlements has been documented by archaeologists in extraordinary detail and precision. Three hundred house sites have been located, with their in- and outlying dependent structures, their churches, chapels, and cemeteries. The contents provide text and map of life in intimate detail. Verbal chronicles are somewhat meager after the initial period of settlement.

The boundary between productive and unproductive land was more sharply drawn than in volcanic Iceland. The ice cap that covers Greenland exposes a narrow and discontinuous fringe of land along the seacoast. Only at the southwest is there a body of soil, formed of the waste of glacier and sediment of water, that supports vegetation useful to man, mainly in strips and patches about fjords. During his exile Eric familiarized himself with all the habitable coast, consisting of the two districts that became the Eastern and Western Settlements. He selected for himself the estate he named Brattahlid at the head of the fjord he named Eiriksfjord after himself. About it and the fjord adjacent to the east, most of the homesteads of the Eastern Settlement were located, their meadows on low ground, the pastures on stony hillsides. Brattahlid and nearby Gardar, seat of the bishop, were the best and largest properties, the hub of the colony. The Western Settlement, with a colder climate and smaller and poorer patches of soil, lacked a similar nucleus.

As in Iceland, most homesteads were chosen because they were thought suitable for animal husbandry. Once the animal shelters were built that were necessary for the cold winters and a palatable herbage was established by burning and by improved drainage, the farmstead was soon at the limit of its productivity. The growing season was shorter than in Iceland, the possibility of cutting and storing hay probably less. Under such circumstances the hungering stock of necessity was turned out as new growth became available in spring, with cumulative injury to the pastures. The newly thawed and wet ground was trampled, cut, and puddled by hooves, and put into poor condition for summer growth. Also, erosion by wind and water set in, as Roussell's study of farmsteads has made evident.

Animal husbandry was carried on as the accustomed way of life rather than because it was rewarding economically. The production of milk and meat was meager and declined in time under the sharp restriction of seasons and productive land. Refuse heaps thus record diminishing dependence on domestic animals. These continued to provide wool, leather, and horn to maintain Norse habits and skills.

Graves of the latest period show that the Greenlanders dressed in wool to the end of the colony.

The inner fjords about which most of the homesteads lay were least advantageous for fishing, hunting, and fowling. This was especially true of the Western Settlement, where glacial meltwaters and sediment discharge into all fjord heads. For both settlements the prospect for a greater supply of food and other necessities lay in the lower fjords and on the outer headlands and islands. Bones of seal are the most abundant item in the refuse of homesteads, even in those farthest from the sea. Husbandry alone could not maintain the people and probably did so less and less.

## THE OPENING TO THE NORTHWEST

Both settlements began early to send boat parties on hunting expeditions to the Nordrsetr, about and above Davis Strait. Here seals were found in largest number and here was the range of Arctic animals that came only on occasion as far south as the settlements, walrus, narwhals and other small whales, and polar bears. The Greenland Annals of 1267 told that seal hunting was better in the north than in the settlements and described how the rendered seal fat was poured into sacks of hide hung against the wind until it thickened, and was then stowed for transport south.[1]

This far northern back country, annually visited but not inhabited, filled out the life of the Greenlanders by adding diversity of product to change of experience. Vilhjalmur Stefansson considered Nordrsetr "a kind of hunting vacation from the more prosaic southerly farms."[2] As the driftwood was used up on the settled coasts, its final deposit about Disko Bay became needed. It was prime country for sea

[1] Nansen, vol. 1, p. 293.
[2] Vilhjalmur Stefansson, *The Three Voyages of Martin Frobisher*, vol. 1 (London, 1938), pp. lx–lxii; also Tryggvi Oleson, *Early Voyages and Northern Approaches* (London, 1964), pp. 40–41.

mammals and there were also caribou, hares, and Arctic foxes to hunt and eider down to collect.

Eider ducks may provide a sort of record of how far north the Greenlanders ranged in these Arctic seas, as Stefansson explained. Arctic explorers of the nineteenth century and since have found crude stone structures far to the north, as in Smith and Jones sounds that connect Baffin Bay with the Arctic Ocean. Some are cairns, apparently ancient, but others are miniature boxlike structures of stone. The latter were described in the Nares expedition of 1875 as "four stones piled together like a miniature 'Druid altar,' so as to form a chamber large enough to shelter a nest." Otto Sverdrup saw them in his expedition of 1899–1902, in an uninhabited country which they were "the first civilized people to visit," and thought they had been built by Eskimos, but was bothered by two thoughts, one that he had never heard of Eskimos thus protecting eider ducks, the other that this was the practice in northernmost Norway in his time. Stefansson found thereby the key, as he said, to distinguish Norse from Eskimo presence, the Eskimos protecting no birds and killing eider ducks whenever they could and using their skins. "In Norse communities it is anti-social, if not a crime, to kill eiders or destroy their eggs." In order to attract eiders to nest so that their down might be gathered, the Norse built such shelters, carefully protecting the birds and eggs. These duck "houses" and cairns, found north beyond Baffin Bay, thus identify the entry of Greenlanders into latitudes not reached again by Europeans until the nineteenth century.

## DEPENDENCE ON NORDRSETR

The trips into the farther north were more than hunting vacations. From Eastern to Western Settlement it is more than three hundred miles, thence on to Disko Bay nearly four hundred more, and to Upernivik another two hundred. Near the latter place, a rune stone was found which told that three men had erected cairns in April of the year 1333(?), in other words, had overwintered there. From Upernivik on to Smith Sound it is about five hundred miles farther, as it is also by another route to Jones Sound, both of which apparently were reached by Norse. Their farthest distance north from the Greenland settlements is comparable to voyaging between Greenland and Norway.

The northern driftwood was increasingly desired as the southern supplies became used up. Stefansson has made a case for eiderdown collected from nesting places that the Norsemen prepared. The main importance of the north was that it provided things of price with which to buy merchandise from Europe. For a time there was strong demand in Europe for walrus ivory. Baffin Bay became the major walrus ground of the time, Arctic Europe having been much depleted. Walrus ivory and walrus hides were principal exports from Greenland. The tusks of narwhal of Baffin Bay also furnished ivory and were highly prized in medieval medicine. Sealskins and seal oil were available in quantity in Nordrsetr. Stefansson called attention to the white falcons, mainly found about Baffin Bay, as most prized by medieval falconry. These were carried to Europe, where they brought a high price. The item of greatest luxury was the polar bear. Taken as cubs, they were presented by Norwegian and Danish kings to rulers such as Henry III of England and Emperor Frederick II. One found its way to the sultan of Egypt. Bear traps are said to be found as far north as Smith and Jones sounds. Polar bears almost exclusively, white falcons mainly, and eider ducks largely were available to the Norsemen in the coasts and waters from Davis Strait north to Ellesmere Land, the farthest Nordrsetr.[3] The luxury items

---

[3] Stefansson, pp. xlii–xliv, and Oleson, pp. 36–43, largely after Jon Duason.

of the far north, not the hides and wool of the settlements, gave the Greenlanders such purchasing power as they had.

## THE FALLING OFF OF SEAFARING

The settlers brought their own ships and boats when they came to Greenland. For the most part these had been brought to Iceland from Europe. The Greenland colonists were a humbler lot and of less property than those who had settled Iceland. Their sagas lack the proud genealogies of Iceland and of the Faeroes. Very few had capital to draw upon such as many vikings took to Iceland. Homesteads could be built by hard work, but ships and boats were another matter. As these were lost, worn out, or needed serious repair they could be replaced only by purchase. A shortage of ships is inferred as early as the Vinland sagas. Leif bought a ship from Bjarni Herjolfsson, who made his living trading between Norway and Iceland. The Greenland Saga makes this ship serve for five Vinland voyages. Karlsefni, a "very well to do man," and another Icelander brought their wares on two ships to Eiriksfjord and then went in them to Vinland. Cunning Freydis persuaded two Icelander brothers, also traders between Norway and Greenland, to add their ship to her venture. From the beginning the commerce of Greenland was carried by ships belonging to Icelanders or Norwegians.

The store of driftwood did not take care of all needs. The settlers were not shipwrights. The stranded wood was softwood, spruce, fir, and poplar, not the oak and ash needed for frames and oars. As the southern supplies were reduced, timber had to be brought from the north, as from Disko Bay, by long and difficult haul. They might thus repair boats but they were not able to build or service shipyards. A lone small Greenland-built ship is of record as having been to Markland, storm-driven to Iceland in 1347.

The sea hunting expeditions to Nordrsetr continued for

more than three centuries, in the course of which it was necessary to replace boats and ships repeatedly. Gradually the costs exceeded the returns. Fewer parties went north; contacts between the two settlements also became exceptional; the people were more and more landlocked. The wool and hides of the homesteads were needed at home and were hardly competitive in foreign markets. The products from Nordrsetr became costlier to procure and the demand became less. In the mid-thirteenth century the well-informed King's Mirror reported that ships seldom went to Greenland and that whatever was taken there from other lands was dear, mentioning iron and tar and things needed for houses. In other words, there were no longer enough things of value produced in Greenland to repay visits by merchant ships. In 1276 the Archbishop of Nidaros in Norway, in charge of collecting tithes from Greenland, wrote the pope that it might take five years to collect these and then they would be paid in leather and leather rope (of walrus?) for which there was but a poor market.

Nansen remarked on the increasing isolation as bringing "hard conditions at the extreme limit at which a European culture was possible; it wanted little to turn the scale. It is therefore easy to understand that as soon as communication with the mother country declined, the conditions of life in Greenland became so unattractive that those who had the chance removed elsewhere."[4] This condition was chronic by the thirteenth century. The land was insufficient to support the population, and the sea had become less and less accessible because boats cost too much. The salable harvest of the Nordrsetr seas fell off to a degree that reduced Norwegian commerce almost to nothing and raised prices of imports. The commercial economy had broken down and the subsistence economy was inadequate.

[4] This and the following quotes are from Nansen, ch. 11.

# FAILURE OF THE GREENLAND SETTLEMENTS

Greenland and Iceland surrendered their independence in 1261, expecting Norway to provide them with sufficient service of ships. The result was the opposite, with new restrictions of trade and new taxes. The church became the principal owner of property in Greenland. In 1294 the crown made the Greenland trade a royal monopoly that was rented out to Norwegian merchants. "Only the King's ships—and of these there was as a rule only one, called 'Knarren,' for the Greenland traffic—were permitted to sail there for the purposes of trade, and this was the beginning of the end." This service became more and more irregular and apparently stopped before 1370. Greenland became dependent at first on Iceland for merchant ships. In turn Iceland depended on supplies by ships operating out of Norway. During the fourteenth century Norway experienced a disastrous decline of its shipping, had great political troubles, and was stricken by the plague. The settlers remaining in Greenland were isolated and almost forgotten. The last Norwegian ship recorded as having sailed to Greenland did so in 1410.

## DISAPPEARANCE OF THE SETTLEMENTS

The Western Settlement received little attention in the chronicles. More has been learned about it through recent archaeologic work. Its homesteads for the most part were small and meager. The northern group was under the greater necessity to go on sea hunts, and they were better situated to go to the rewarding northern coasts. The Western Settlement lasted for about three hundred and fifty years and then disappeared, apparently suddenly, without record of what happened. The larger Eastern Settlement, with more and better land, continued for another hundred and fifty years, the last century of which is known mainly by archaeologic determination.

The fourteenth century was one of progressive decline

147

and retreat. Its scanty records have been little altered since
Nansen wrote his eleventh chapter, as here abstracted:

1330 (ca.): The rune stone at Upernivik (72° 47' N.)
was carved by a party that overwintered there.

1342: According to the seventeenth-century Annals of
the  Icelandic Bishop Gisli Oddson, this was the year
when the Western Settlement "voluntarily forsook the
true faith and the religion of the Christians, and after
having abandoned all good morals and true virtues,
turned to the people of America (*ad Americae populos se converterunt*)." The same event and time are told
in a fourteenth-century history preserved in a later
manuscript: "Now the Skraelings possess the whole
Western Settlement; there are indeed horses, goats,
cattle and sheep, all wild, and no people either Christian
or heathen . . . all this is told by Ivar Bardsson, a
Greenlander, who was steward of the bishop's residence at Gardar in Greenland for many years, that he
had seen all this and he was one of those chosen by the
'lagmand' to go to the Western Settlement against the
Skraelings to expel the Skraelings from the Western
Settlement and when they came there they found no
man, either Christian or heathen, but some wild cattle
and sheep, and ate of the wild cattle, and took as much
as the ships could carry and sailed with it home." (Ivar
was steward at Gardar, the bishop's seat in the Eastern
Settlement, around the middle of the century and would
have been a proper person to look into the condition
of the north. It is implied that the major settlement had
been out of touch with the northern one, which was
thought to have been entered or taken over by Eskimos.
Instead they found no people but livestock in abundance. The account was confused, Nansen pointing out

correctly that unattended livestock could not have survived a winter, and also that, had Eskimos been there, being hunters they would not have spared the livestock and removed the Greenlanders. There are other, still vaguer references to the loss of the Western Settlement.)

1347: the previously noted arrival in Iceland of a small Greenland ship that had been to Markland and had been driven off its course.

1379: by notice in another Annal, that "the Skraelings harried the Greenlanders and killed of them sixteen men and took two boys and made slaves of them."

1385–7: a Norwegian, Björn Einarsson, known as Jerusalem Farer, was storm-driven west into Eiriksfjord, where he spent two years before being able to return to Norway. The party were well provided for by the Greenlanders and were given a hundred and fifty sheep at their departure. Björn saved two Eskimo children ("trolls") who had been stranded on a skerry at the entry to the fjord. These "were skilled in all kinds of hunting" and thus occupied themselves for their hosts. They became so attached to Björn that they threw themselves into the sea when he left.

This, in sum, is what is of record of the fourteenth century as to the loss of the Western Settlement and the appearance of Eskimos in the Eastern Settlement. The latter was last noted as visited by a ship in 1410, the cemetery at Herjolfsness giving evidence however that some Norse lived to the end of the fifteenth century.

## ATTACKS UPON THE SETTLEMENTS?

That the unwarlike Eskimos should have driven the Greenlanders back and finally eliminated them by force is quite out of character for both groups. Nansen found it necessary to object to such claims (cited above for 1379) as contrary to the ways of the Eskimos, who did not carry on offensive warfare, or capture or keep slaves. The assertion was made almost three centuries after the supposed event, on unknown authority, and is improbable.

It is suggested that the Eastern Settlement was harried by raids of European "pirates." Slave trading was a not uncommon part of the commerce of the time. Clandestine trade in particular might pick up such cargo, whether of heathens or Christians. By the fifteenth century Hanseatic and English ships were trafficking to Iceland. In 1413 King Eric of Norway protested to Henry V of England against unlawful trade with outlying parts of his realm. Complaint was again made in 1431, naming acts of violence and rapine by which many persons had perished. Iceland was given as the main sufferer, but Greenland was also mentioned. The following year the English king signed a treaty engaging to make good the losses and to return the people who had been carried off during the preceding twenty years. These acts give credence to a letter attributed to Pope Nicholas V as of 1448, citing a fleet of barbarians who had cruelly attacked Greenland thirty years earlier and had carried away inhabitants of both sexes as slaves, most of whom were later returned to their homes. Egil Thorhallessen (1776) was cited by Stefansson as of the opinion that these barbarians were not Eskimos but Englishmen; he also cited Gustav Meldorf as saying that Greenlanders who escaped the pirates were befriended by Eskimos.[5]

## AD AMERICAE POPULOS

When Eric came to Greenland it was uninhabited. The first sight of native people probably came elsewhere, in the

[5] Stefansson, pp. xxxii, xlix–1, lxix; Nansen, pp. 114–118.

150

# FAILURE OF THE GREENLAND SETTLEMENTS

Vinland voyages. At about that time, Eskimos began to move from the Arctic islands of Canada into farthest north-western Greenland. These were remarkably skilled hunters and trappers competent to sustain themselves in an Arctic environment, on land and sea and along the seasonally changing water's edge. Archaeologists have named them the Thule Culture. Gradually and slowly they moved south along the west coast of Greenland, where the littoral of the Baffin Sea and Davis Strait gave excellent and diverse hunting. This was the Nordrsetr that the Greenlanders visited on summer hunting parties and where some occasionally over-wintered. Greenlanders and Eskimos, thus first came into contact in the north. Norse elements have been found in Thule sites. Norse hunters found some native habitations in the Disko region. The descendants of Thule, the Inugsuk Eskimo, continued to move south as seal hunters and fowlers, perhaps of late record in the troll children who were picked up by Björn the Jerusalem Farer. Nansen noted that there was no contest for territory involved; as the Eskimo moved south they lived along the open coast, the Greenlanders re-mained in the inner parts of the fjords.

Whether contact with the Norse contributed new en-ergy to the Eskimo that urged them to occupy more and more of the Greenland coast is uncertain. The Eskimos were in superior balance with the environment. The Greenlanders continued to apply themselves to a meager animal husbandry of diminishing returns. That they were excessively slow to adapt their habits is shown by the cemeteries in which the Christian Norse to the last were buried, dressed in woolen clothes of European style.

The decline of the colony had become serious in the thirteenth century, as was shown by the critical shortage of shipping. By the next century the Greenlanders were reduced to a shrinking subsistence economy. The Western Settlement had disappeared, the Eastern one would linger to the end of the fifteenth century in a manner so obscure that it is known only through some fortunately preserved graves and by European complaints about slaves. In the seventeenth century an Icelandic bishop, writing of the Western Settlement said that the people had voluntarily forsaken the Christian faith, "ad Americae populos se converterunt." This Stefansson translated as "amalgamated themselves with the people of America." The bishop's epitaph on the Greenlanders has the merit of brevity, synopsis, and lament. It does not tell whom it considered the people of America nor whether it placed Greenland in America. At that time fishermen from Europe were frequenting Newfoundland and English captains were seeking a Northwest Passage. There is an intimation that the bishop may have thought of a Norse transfer across Davis Strait. At any rate a century after the extinction of the Greenland settlements it was believed in Iceland that the Greenlanders had been absorbed into native stock and ways.

The thesis that the last of the Greenlanders were assimilated into Eskimos was accepted by Nansen and connected by him with the deterioration of their economic condition and the loss of communication with Iceland and Norway.

> The settlements in Greenland almost entirely cut off must have decayed; comparatively few, perhaps were able to get passage, and left the country by degrees; but the people declined in numbers; they adopted an entirely Eskimo mode of living, and mixed with the Eskimos, who perhaps spread southwards in greater numbers along the west coast of Greenland . . . When they were reduced, without any support from Europe, to make the best of the country's resources; then the real superiority of the Eskimo in these surroundings asserted its full rights, and the Greenlanders had to begin to look upon them in a very different light. It is therefore perfectly natural that from this very fourteenth century a fundamental change in the relation between Norsemen and Skraelings set in.

Stefansson agreed and found that it had been advanced

by others before Nansen. Egil Thorhallessen, who had been in Greenland in 1774–5, found evidence against the killing off of the Greenlanders by Eskimos, Black Death, or hunger and concluded that they had been assimilated into the Eskimos. Eilert Sund wrote in 1860: "When the connection with the mother-country stopped so that the Norwegians had to get along without such things as iron for tools and clergymen for the maintenance of divine service, it will be understood that the Norwegian culture and way of life was no longer possible. But it was possible to live in the Eskimo manner." Sund then had "the embarrassing thought" that a Norwegian girl might come to prefer an Eskimo kayak paddler as the better support of a family.[6]

The Western Settlement, poorest in land and nearest to the northern hunting country, had most numerous contacts with Eskimos, at first in the north and gradually on their own shores, and thus was first to be absorbed. The last trace of Norse in the Eastern Settlement gives evidence of Christian burial in European dress and of unmixed Nordic breed. Stefansson concluded: "Those who liked hunting would no doubt stay in the north, while the misfits (from the hunter point of view) returned to the peasant life of the Eastern Settlement. In that sense the most southerly districts of Greenland were being subjected to a reverse natural selection. The adventurous, those of restless energy, the pioneer type, would have been gradually eliminated by migration leaving behind the conservative, and, in certain respects, the weaker."[7]

The acceptable thesis that the remnant Greenlanders were assimilated into a viable Eskimo stock and culture has been stretched into an extreme version by Tryggvi Oleson, after Jon Duason; they describe the Tunnit, a people of Eski-

---

[6] Quoted by Stefansson, pp. lxviii–lxx.
[7] Stefansson, pp. xxviii–xxxii.

mo legend as Norsemen, who crossed with the Eskimos and produced the Thule archaeology.

The Icelanders who followed Eric to Greenland found a land quite as attractive as the one they had left. Fishing was as good; driftwood more abundant. Nordrsetr afforded much better hunting at sea and alongshore than did Iceland, and also the hunting of land game. The Greenlanders, like their kindred elsewhere, became attached to their homesteads. Of these there were about three hundred, a hundred of which were classed as cots or other minor sites.[8] Eric's Brattahlid and the bishop's seat at Gardar were estates of some extent and pretension, as were perhaps two or three others. There was no more land to be put to use, and the ampler resources of the sea were increasingly beyond their capacities. The population grew smaller and poorer, more isolated and less enterprising. They were too few, too remote, too little diversified in skills to improve or even to maintain their condition. Their own limitations of knowledge and habits in an exacting environment—one may say their cultural rigidity—explains the course of their decline.

Some students have sought to put importance on physical degeneration. Emigration, as Stefansson said, was counterselective by removing the more vigorous and venturesome stock. Skeletal studies have been presented as showing an enfeebled population in the late period, but the evidence has also been challenged.[9] Nansen thought that the Norse, deprived of grain and increasingly so of milk, became poorly nourished, whereas the Eskimos by long selection had become adapted to an animal diet. In this respect Stefansson disagreed strongly. In his writings and lecture tours on the Friendly Arctic, as he called it, he exhibited himself as an

[8] Roussell, p. 12.
[9] Summary in Tryggvi Oleson, ch. 11.

example that one could live well and vigorously by hunting and fishing. The Greenlanders lacked neither, nor is there good reason to ascribe their decline to nutritional deficiencies.

## CLIMATIC CHANGE?

There is a present tendency to attribute the Greenland failure to adverse change of climate. A dramatic statement is by Gwyn Jones, who has said that the Norseman, "wedded to his flocks and herds and wasting pastures, could not survive his *fimbulvetr*, that long and awful unremitting winter whose present onset, had he but known it, heralded the ending of his world." "Against the immense and reserved authority of Fridtjof Nansen and Vilhjalmur Stefansson" he cited a representative list in support of climatic crisis.[10]

The thesis that Greenland became uninhabitable to Europeans derives mainly from studies of climatic change in northern Europe during the Middle Ages. Chronicles reported years when crops failed, years without a summer, bad series of years. Analysis of pollen beneath bogs and lakes has shown changes in frequency or presence of pollen of different plants. Thus there has been inferred a "climatic optimum" for northern Europe from the eleventh to the thirteenth century, followed by a "cold" time that gave way to more genial conditions in the fifteenth century. However, there are also increasing reservations about translating such pollen "spectra" into graphs of climate.

The higher latitudes are especially subject to climatic oscillations by reason of changes in the storm tracks that cross them. Movements of polar air masses may follow the same pattern for a number of years. The climate thus may be more "oceanic" for a time, less frigid in winter and cloud-

[10] Jones, pp. 55–61.

ier and cooler in summer. Or it may be more "continental," with greater extremes of temperature and more sun. When Greenland was settled northern Europe is thought to have enjoyed a run of years of "favorable" weather, followed by a turn to colder and wet summers. The data are not extensive for northern Europe, and their extension to the west side of the Atlantic is questionable. If there was a "deterioration" of the climate of Greenland, Roussell thought "it may have started already in the later decades of Norsemen times,"[11] that is, well after the decline of population was far advanced.

One inference is that the increased severity of the climate made it impossible to have enough feed for the livestock on which the Norse depended. They were wedded to their flocks, as Jones has said. Nansen thought that a climatic change did not occur and that, had there been such a change, sea hunting would have improved. Importance has been given to the finds of permanently frozen ground on certain cemetery and house sites. If this means lowered temperatures, it applies to the time after the Norse had gone. Permafrost is also dependent on drainage and thus is favored by increasing and spreading wetness of ground. Under Norse occupation, drainage and aeration of the soil were improved by baring and compacting surfaces, in some cases by ditches. With their disappearance wild vegetation recovered the ground with turf, heath, and moor, forming a water-holding mat over a frozen base. In addition to human intervention drainage has been affected by changes in sea level. "In the course of the excavation of Sandnes farm in the Western Settlement it was found that the church there now lies a good way below the high-water mark, and its lowest part is scarcely dry at the lowest ebb. There are other ruins, in both settlements, which now are half under water, so that a minimum

[11] Roussell, p. 9.

of 5 metres must be reckoned for the [local] submergence that has taken place since mediaevel times."[12]

The arguments that the settlements failed because the climate changed seem incompetent or irrelevant. They failed as far and small outposts that slowly lost the ability to live in the European manner.

[12] Roussell, p. 15.

# CHAPTER VIII   IRISH SEAFARING

*CHRISTIAN IRELAND*

Ireland alone of western Europe was beyond Roman rule or invasion. Late in the fourth century its pagan chieftains raided across the Irish Sea into Roman Britain to return home with loot and slaves, among them a young Christian Briton to become known as St. Patrick. The lands all about the Irish Sea were inhabited by Celtic peoples affiliated in language and instructed in the natural philosophy and mysticism of the Druid Order. Christianity found the Celtic soil congenial, earliest among Britons and Welsh. Ireland became devoutly Christian in the fifth century, without violence or compulsion. Celtic Christianity, with a personality of its own, thrived about and beyond the Irish Sea. Its religious men moved freely by sea between Ireland and Wales, Cumbria, Gaul, and much farther.

Ireland was a fortunate land, remaining untouched by invasions until the end of the eighth century. While the continent and England experienced rude conquests and displacements of people, the Irish practiced works of peace, the cultivation of learning, poetry and music, the maintenance of crafts. Celts had been great metalworkers in antiquity, first on the continent and then in the British Isles. In Ireland they secured copper and gold in the highlands, iron in bogs, and tin from their kinsmen in Cornwall. They continued to excel as artificers in metals both precious and base. In the early Middle Ages Ireland was peaceable, creative, and learned, a light to western Europe.

Irish Christianity developed a direction of its own.

There being no cities and scarcely anything that might be called a town, religious ministration was carried on by monks, some gathered in monasteries, some moving from place to place (these known as *peregrini*), and some withdrawn as hermits into solitary places. A monk might change from one mode of life to the other. Monasteries were the centers of religious and intellectual life. A community of monks with its abbot included scholars versed in Latin and in classical knowledge, spiritual advisers, and men competent in practical affairs. The abbot, often of noble birth and means, gathered about him a following which included lay dependents and associates and their families. Parent monasteries sent out groups to found others, a process of hiving that gave rise to a monastic geography surviving in saints' place names, perpetuating the manner of such proliferation. It was a loosely coherent system, based not on central hierarchy but on the initiative of individual missioners, the bearers of Ireland's golden age.

## IRISH MONKS ABROAD

The first exchange of monks was with Welsh monasteries, but soon Irish monks were also going into Brittany. In the sixth century they were moving in number across the Frankish lands to bring or revive the Christian faith among German tribes from the upper Rhine to the Danube. St. Columbanus led his group by way of Luxeuil in the Vosges to the upper Rhine and across southern Bavaria, St. Gallus to the Swiss canton that bears his name, St. Kilian northeast across south Germany to the valley of the Main, and St. Ferghil (Vergilius), who was accused by St. Boniface of teaching that the earth is round, to found the monastery at Salzburg. Irish missionaries continued to go into the southern German lands well into the eighth century and are remembered there as its Christian apostles.

From the north of Ireland began an Irish colonization

159

of Scotland, where the Irish became known as Scots. Ahead of it went St. Columba and his monks. The abbey he built in 563 on the sacred isle of Iona was the base from which Christianity was taken to the western Scottish lowlands and in a great and rapid sweep through the Hebrides and the north of Scotland to the Orkney Islands. This took place before the end of the sixth century and reached the Shetland Islands early in the seventh. The Pictish natives were converted, and the Irish settled beside them. This Celtic migration lapped all about the north of the British Isles, mingling with the Picts. History tells little of the skills at sea by which this peaceful colonization was carried out. Monks, common folk, and nobles took part. Monasteries were built and empty islands were occupied by hermits who withdrew to the "desert of the sea."

## IMMRAM AND CURRAGH

Christian Ireland from its beginnings lived in a special awareness of the sea, not a sea to be feared or to try the limits of man's courage but which stirred the imagination and drew men to seek what lay beyond the far horizon. Its holy men went innocently into the unknown sea to experience nearness to God and learn his wonders. Being somewhat learned in the classics they knew the Mediterranean legends of the sea, such as of the Fortunate Isles which were thought to lie in the western ocean. Bits of such lore did get woven into their own sea tales but they are not their origin nor do they give the stamp to the Irish sea legends. They are older than Christianity and acquire Christian form that retains an older Celtic world outlook.

This particular Irish literary genre, the immram, deals with high-spirited ventures into the unknown ocean. It is not concerned with battle, hardship, or shipwreck, but with adventure sought and enjoyed, with a seaworld of marvels and

160

incidental terrors ending in safe return. However fantastic the adventures and imaginary the geography, the immram record experiences that were real. Unlike the Norse sagas, they are not concerned with heroism, fate, or family.

Two of the older sea tales are the voyages of Bran and of Mael Duin. The *Voyage of Bran* is thought to have been written at a monastery; its hero bears the name of a Celtic god and is himself a pagan. Bran sails west by curragh to an Island of Joy and then to the Island of Women, beyond which he does not pass, although he knows "There are thrice fifty islands in the ocean to the west." On his return after centuries a member of the crew turns to dust as he steps ashore; Bran then turns back to sea. In the *Voyage of Mael Duin* a Druid advises the building of a curragh for sixty men. Mael Duin exceeds the number by taking three foster brothers, for which disobedience to Druid counsel he meets with adventures on twenty-nine islands. The first foster brother is killed at one. The second remains to weep at an island of mourners. The third remains to laugh on an island where the people laugh all the time. After the crew is reduced to the prescribed number, the ban ends and Mael Duin is able to return home.[1]

Other romances of the sea are concerned with lives of saints, such as Columba, Brendan, and Malo, the oldest being the *Life of St. Columba* by Adamnan. Adamnan was abbot at Iona in the late seventh century and wrote there of the founding of that first monastery north of Ireland. Of St. Brendan there is both a *Life* and a *Navigation*, and of the Welsh St. Malo (Machutus) a *Life*. These were holy men of the sixth century who later became celebrated in legendary biographies of facts, fantasies, Celtic myths, and classical lore. The saintly voyages continue in the tradition of the immram, obscure as to underlying reality but telling of Irish

---

[1] Geoffrey Ashe, *Land to the West* (New York, 1962), ch. 2.

experience of the western sea. Nansen was so bemused by Irish sea legends that he came to suspect the Vinland sagas as largely thus derived, by way of Norsemen who had lived in Ireland.

In the Irish tales of seafaring the curragh is the usual vessel. Niall of the Nine Hostages, from whom the high kings of Tara descended, thus raided Britain and brought St. Patrick to Ireland. The immram voyages were made by curraghs, those of the saints mainly so. The name (coracle as variant) is common to the Celtic peoples of the British Isles, and is applied to a boat of wicker frame covered with hide. In its simplest form it is a round, broad, keelless bowl. It may be given the shape of an elongated, round-bottomed basket. This primitive and ancient boat was retained and developed by the Celts of the British Isles. It needed no selected, dressed, and seasoned timbers but was woven and lashed out of green withes and branches for which native willows, alder, birch, and yew provided the supple and strong materials. Cowhides were stretched over the frame, sewed together, the seams made watertight, and the skins waterproofed with fat. The craft was light, easily beached, and readily repaired. It rode with the waves and did not capsize nor ship water readily. It may have been most uncomfortable in a rough sea, but it was not likely to go under. The curraghs were rowed, worked with sweeps, and sailed with stepped masts. The ones still in use are small fishing boats; in olden times they were built to large dimensions for the transport of people, goods, and livestock.

The curragh is the vessel of Irish tradition. Ireland was not a land of forest in historic time. By the early Middle Ages its use of timber was less than in other parts of Atlantic Europe. There were, however, some wooden ships and boats also. Adamnan in his *Life of St. Columba* mentioned among several kinds of vessels long ships of hewn pine and oak.[2] Until the vikings drove the Irish from the high seas they were active seafarers, along with other Celtic peoples the earliest westerners thus engaged.

## THE NAVIGATION OF ST. BRENDAN

St. Brendan (or Brandon) was born about 484 and may have lived to 577, his time being that of the first generation of Irish missionaries who went out to other lands. His place of birth was a castle on the Bay of Tralee, beyond which Brandon Mountain, Brandon Head, and Brandon Bay carry his name as patron saint of County Kerry. The outlook is west into the open Atlantic. A short distance north of Tralee he built the monastery of Ardfert, of which he was abbot. With some of his family of monks he went for a time to the famed Welsh monastery of Llancarfan in the Vale of Glamorgan, where St. Malo became his pupil and from which they went together on an expedition at sea, by tradition a far voyage. Late in life he built another monastery at Clonfert in central Ireland, before which he had been to the Hebrides and perhaps also had built another monastery on Coney Island in the River Shannon. At some time he had engaged in discourse with other religious in Brittany. At the age of eighty he was again in the Hebrides. These are the reasonably assured facts of his life, long stretches being unaccounted for.

The legend of St. Brendan began to appear early in the ninth century, first in liturgical matter, as in a litany invoking the aid of the sixty who had gone with him in quest of the Land of Promise. By the next century the legend had taken form in two related versions, the *Life* and the *Navigation*, both to be widely circulated by Irish peregrini outside of

[2] Ashe, p. 71.

Ireland. To his countrymen he became the patron saint of navigators. The experiences and sights related in the *Navigation* include the Christian myth of the Earthly Paradise and also classical lore of the Fortunate Islands. They were composed before the Norse knew of Vinland or Greenland, and Nansen was of the opinion that they colored the Norse sagas.

The *Navigation* has been regarded by some as fantasy, by others as chiefly myth with descriptions that may have rested on real observations. Geoffrey Ashe has made a bold and ingenious attempt to arrange its geography as actually applying from the Arctic Ocean to the West Indies. Nothing being known of the completed tale until three centuries after St. Brendan, it is likely to have had woven into it later knowledge of the sea. Thus the Sheep Island and the Paradise of Birds may well have been islands of the Faeroes. Whether St. Brendan visited them is another matter. At the time when the legend came into vogue the Irish had been driven from the seas by the vikings. The *Navigation* recalled the olden times when they had been free to rove the seas, the past embodied in St. Brendan as its culture hero. However embellished by miraculous, edifying, and allegorical events and poetically contrived, the two Brendan tales have the quality of experience in distant seas.

According to the *Life* the monks built three great curraghs at the foot of Brandon Mountain and equipped them with sails and oars, each boat capable of holding thirty men. For five years they visited island after island. On their return his foster-mother St. Ita told Brendan that he would never reach the sanctified country, where no blood is shed, in a boat made of slaughtered skins. He accordingly moved to Connaught, where he built a large wooden ship.[3] (An in-

[3] Ashe, pp. 64–65.

dication that there was still proper timber in northwestern Ireland and that wooden ships were being made?)

The *Navigation* begins with a story a monk told Brendan of having voyaged to an island guarded by an angel, which was the Earthly Paradise. This decided Brendan to assemble his monks at the foot of Brandon Mountain, where they built a curragh with wicker sides and ribs, covered it with cowhide tanned in oak bark, and tarred the seams. They used butter to dress the hides. They sailed the western sea for years, going in different directions, seeing islands great and small, some wondrous, others fearsome. From time to time they met ancient Irish hermits.

The historical Brendan was a founder of monasteries, a teacher and missionary in Scotland, Wales, and Brittany, probably at times a hermit. By Breton tradition he went on a voyage with his pupil Machutus (St. Malo) in search of the Isle of the Blessed. Of all Irish saints he was the most celebrated as a navigator. The tradition had basis in facts, the nature of which is shrouded in legend. The time was that of Ireland's greatest cultural vigor, when Irishmen set out to sea on high and holy endeavor.

## THE ISLES OF THE BLESSED

In medieval Christian tradition the lost Earthly Paradise lay in the farthest East. In older classical lore the Fortunate Islands or blessed lands were in the western ocean. The Celtic Otherworld also lay to the west. Cardinal directions have deep religious significance, differing by particular culture. The premise is offered that Irish pre-Christian mysticism looked to the west as the promised land or other world, and that this direction held into Christian time.

The Atlantic Ocean of the Middle Ages was thought strewn with islands, some imagined as places of perfect

165

nature and as abodes of the blessed, either spirits or living persons. The legendary islands acquired widely known names when cartographers began to transfer stories of the sea to their maps. From the thirteenth century on, island names appeared on maps in increasing numbers and in changing locations, to the distress of modern historians of cartography.

Other than the Fortunate Islands, which were the dimly remembered reality of the Canary Islands, the oldest and most persistent island names on maps derive from Celtic sources. Insofar as I know the oldest of these is Yma, the isle of the blessed named in the *Life of St. Machutus*, which St. Brendan and St. Malo set out to find. In variant spellings the name appears on maps of the fourteenth century and through the fifteenth, by which time it had become one of the Antilles.[4]

Honorius of Autun in his *De Imagine Mundi* (*ca.* 1130) added the island Perdita: "There lies in the Ocean an island which is called the Lost (Perdita); in charm and all kinds of fertility it far surpasses every other land, but is unknown to men. Now and again it may be found by chance; but if one seeks for it, it cannot be found and therefore is called 'the Lost.' Men say that it was this island that Brandanus came to."[5] The Ebstorf Map (1270?) entered an *Insula perdita*, with the Latin inscription, "This is the island found by Saint Brendan, and after he sailed for it, never after has it been found by any man." By 1300 the Hereford Map stated that "the Fortunate Islands, six in number, are the islands of St. Brendan."[6] This map maker interpreted St. Brendan's alleged discovery as identical with the Fortunate Islands of antiquity, the Canaries.

These early map makers were wholly ignorant of geo-

---

4 A. Cortesão, pp. 78–80; p. 48.
5 Nansen, vol. 1, p. 376.
6 A. Cortesão, pp. 39–40.

graphical position. The tale of the voyaging of St. Brendan
first passed into chronicle and map in western Europe and
later was taken up by Italian and Catalan cartographers.
Celtic legends provided a major part of the concept of the
western ocean until Prince Henry introduced recorded exploration. As late as 1492 Martin Behaim placed St. Brendan's Isle on his globe in midocean near the equator with
the inscription "In the year 565 A.D. S. Brandon came in his
ship to this island. He saw many marvels there and after
seven years left again for his country."[7] Behaim is remembered mainly for the terrestrial globe he made before the discovery by Columbus, the only such that has survived from
that century; his knowledge was a good deal less than that
of his time.

The most persistent of the legendary islands was that of
Brasil, which had a separate and migratory existence on
maps and later became confused with a name of different
origin and meaning. E. T. Hamy showed in 1887 that Brasil
was from the Gaelic term for fortunate or blessed (*breas-ail,
hy-breasail, o'brasil*, etc.). The vernacular Irish name for the
isle of the blessed is first shown cartographically on the
Italian Dalorto map of 1325, as lying to the west of Ireland.
Thereafter it appears on many maps, Italian and Catalan,
continuing well into the fifteenth century. On the Pizigani
map (1367) it was placed far west in the Atlantic in the
latitude of Brittany. On the Phillipps Chart (1424) it is
shown as a large disk to the west of Ireland and in the same
form on the Pareto map (1455), the latter having also an
island of Mam (Yma?) to the south, in the form of a
crescent.[8]

The earlier locations of Brasil are in the ocean west of
Ireland. This tradition seems to derive from the voyages of

[7] Ravenstein, p. 77.
[8] A. Cortesão for numerous references.

St. Brendan and St. Malo and was kept alive in folk memory. In 1480 Bristol, as previously noted, sent out one Thloyde (Lloyd), the most "knowledgeable seaman of the whole of England" to the "Island of Brasylle" to the west of Ireland. A Welsh mariner who had the knowledge to sail west to the island of Brasil? Another expedition was sent out the following year to find the "Isle of Brasile," and apparently succeeded, as related under the Bristol voyages. Brasil of the Celtic tradition became in fact the new found land, which neither proves nor disproves how far the voyages attributed to St. Brendan got. The tradition was so strong that many centuries later voyages from Bristol set their course west across the Atlantic toward its supposed location.[9]

Late in the fourteenth century map makers began to place an island of Brasil in a different location, guessed at as representing the Azores and even the Canaries. The maps were Italian and Catalan, made in remote reception of Atlantic knowledge and surmise and still ignorant of geographic position. Speculation as to the identity of this island has proposed a derivation from a rootword "bras," flame-colored, as in brazilwood. This dyewood was an item of medieval trade from the Far East but is not native to islands of the eastern Atlantic. It was therefore suggested that the inferred dyewood-island name was applied to islands providing a less vivid dye from lichens. This dye, however, has a name that was familiar at that time, *archil* in its English form, *orseille* in French, *orchilla* in Spanish, and so on. The substitution of brasil for it is unlikely, aside from the doubt that the Azores or Madeira were then known. One might speculate that a place had been discovered thus early where

[9] The island existed in the mind of the British Admiralty into the latter nineteenth century (1873?). An 1869 Maltby globe (in the Department of Geography at Berkeley), made "under the superintendence of the Society for the Diffusion of Useful Knowledge," has a "Brazil Rock High" in the deep ocean about 250 miles west of Tralee.

brazilwood grew. This would have been in the West Indies or South America, which is about as improbable as the lichen attribution.

The preferable option seems to be that the Gaelic name brasil wandered south in the Atlantic by misinformation of Mediterranean map makers, perhaps by misinterpretation of the *Navigation* of St. Brendan or of another Gaelic seafarer such as St. Malo.

The legendary Gaelic isle of the blessed, Brasil, had nothing to do with the naming of the South American country, which was known as Santa Cruz until 1507, when it was given the name Brazil because of its wealth of that dyewood. What facts of discovery may be contained in the legendary voyages of St. Brendan remain unknown.

The promised land of Irish tradition lay in the western ocean, and passed into Christian mythology with St. Brendan as the legendary seafarer. The Irish were indeed the first nation of the Middle Ages to go out onto the high Atlantic. Shortly the mists of legend gave way to historical fact.

## THE FAEROE ISLANDS

The earliest account of the Faeroe Islands is in Dicuil, *De mensura Orbis terrae*, dated about 825:

> There are many other islands to the north of Britain, which can be reached from the northernmost isles of Britain by sailing directly for two days and nights under full sail and with favoring wind. A certain presbyter, a religious, told me that in the course of two summer days and an intervening night, going in a small boat (*navicula*) of two thwarts, he came to one of these. Some of the islands are quite small; most are separated by narrow straits. Hermits who had come from our Scotia have been living in them for about a hundred years. But, as they were always uninhabited from the beginning of the world, so being now vacated by the anchorites on account of the Norse brigands, they are full of innumerable sheep and various kinds of sea fowl. We have never found these islands mentioned in the books of authors.

169

Dicuil was an Irish monk who, like numbers of his kind, went to the Frankish lands where he was a noted scholar. He wrote an astronomy about 815 and the geography *De mensura Orbis terrae* ten years later, probably at the Carolingian court. The treatise testifies to the state of Irish learning. St. Boniface earlier had denounced St. Vergilius (the Irish Ferghil) for teaching the Germans that the Earth was round. Dicuil so declared in the title of his book, supported by a fifth-century authority, Theophrastus' *Mensuratio Orbis*, and by his own observation and reasoning. Also he compiled what he could of regional geography, using reports of traveled Irish monks. One thus told about being on the Nile and going from it by canal to the Red Sea. Another gave the account of the Faeroes cited above. Others told of Iceland, as remains to be noted, with their evidence of the spherical shape of the Earth. Dicuil and his fellow monks were not befogged by myth or doctrine.

The terse relation by the religious informant, meaning a monk, is of sailing from the northernmost British islands, which were the Shetlands, to the Faeroes. Under favorable conditions the distance, close to two hundred miles, was made in two days and nights. The monk made it in a summer voyage in somewhat less time, apparently using a curragh equipped with oars and sail and having a crew experienced in taking the direct course. The Faeroes had been vacated by then by the Irish anchorites because of the appearance of vikings. It is not stated whether this was before or after the visit of the presbyter. The time indicates the end of the eighth century, viking raids hitting Ireland hard from 793 on. Irish hermits had lived on the islands for about a hundred years, implying a succession of holy men who came to this northern retreat throughout the eighth century. Dicuil looked for mention of these islands by older authors, found none, gave them their first written notice with the approximate time of Irish entry, and heard that they had not been previously inhabited. The brief report is factual and competent.

Vikings began to visit the Faeroe Islands before or at the beginning of the ninth century. It appears to have been a half-century later when they came to settle, by which time the islands had acquired their Norse name Faeroe, the sheep islands. Irish religious had stocked a number of the islands with sheep, which had increased greatly in their time and continued to thrive thereafter for a half-century, unattended by man. This increase of sheep was the main attraction for Norse settlement. Extraordinarily mild winters (January mean temperature 4° Centigrade, as in the Shetlands) gave year-round browse and pasture. There were no predators, except possibly eagles. Once established, a breed of sheep already selected for hardiness in the Scottish islands was able to survive and increase.

In this, as in the other Irish relations of seafaring, only the holy men are mentioned. The presbyter said nothing of the seamen who took him by direct and sure passage to the Faeroes. When the hermits went out to seek island retreats they did not go alone, nor was it they who loaded the sheep on the curraghs, stocked the islands, and took care of the sheep. Whatever else than pious contemplation they did, the hermits depended on others to transport them and maintain them. Hermits on the continent were also supported by help from the devout. To reach the Faeroes and continue to live there by replacement "for about a hundred years" implies the skills and services of a supporting lay population.

The presbyter reported that the anchorites had vacated the islands, the time inferred being early in the ninth century, leaving an interval of a half-century before Norse settlement, as supported by the Faeroe Saga. It is not said where the hermits went. That a part of the lay population remained has been suggested, for instance by Nansen. Irish

171

place names in the Faeroes would be thus accounted for, and the ease with which the vikings turned to sheep raising. The people in the south islands are reported as darker and slighter than in the north, indicating a non-Nordic stock, such as Picts, but they may have been brought by Norse settlers coming from Scotland.

## THE IRISH IN ICELAND

The earliest notice again is from Dicuil:

> It is now some thirty years since certain priests, who had been on that island [which he called Thyle] from the first of February to the first of August, told that not only at the time of the summer solstice, but also before and after the setting sun hides itself as it were behind a small mound, so that it does not grow dark even for a short while, but whatsoever a man is doing, even to picking lice out of his shirt, he may do just as though the sun were visible, and had they been on high mountains of the island perhaps the sun would not be concealed at any time.
>
> Those who sailed there arrived at the season of greatest cold; while there they always had alternation of day and night except around the time of the summer solstice; but at a day's sail to the north they found the sea frozen.

This is competent physical geography. Dicuil, proponent of the spherical shape of the Earth, found confirmation by what priests told of the changes in length of day and night during their six months' stay in Iceland. He thus knew that the island lay close to the Arctic Circle. Sailing by way of the Faeroes the normal landfall would be at the southeast of Iceland, as it was later for the Norsemen. Continuing north along the east coast, they would shortly encounter pack or drift ice. The south and southeast coast is not icebound. Dicuil was interested in the voyage because it proved him right as to the shape of the Earth. The priests went to visit, not to discover an unknown land. That they undertook the voyage in midwinter, going more than three hundred miles beyond the Faeroes, makes sense only if they knew the route and that this was a favorable season as to fog and seas.

172

Arriving "at the season of the greatest cold," they stayed for six months, knowing that they would have shelter and food at monastery and cell. Dicuil's reference to the visit as having taken place some thirty years beforehand places it in the latter part of the eighth century. There is no mention of the time when monks first went to Iceland. Dicuil wrote at a time when monks from the British Isles were going there with confidence to visit their kind.

The rest of the information on early Iceland is from Norse sources. Ari the Learned wrote in the *Islendigabok*: "Christians lived here whom the Northmen call 'papa.' Later they went away because they did not wish to live here together with heathen men. They left behind Irish books, bells, and croziers, from which it could be seen that they were Irish." The *Landnamabok* had about the same report. "Before Ireland was settled from Norway, there were people there whom the Northmen called 'papa.' These were Christians and it is thought that they must have been from the British Isles [in another version 'from the west across the sea'], for there were found after their departure Irish books, bells, and croziers, and other things, from which it could be seen that they were Westmen [Norse name for Irish; the *Hauksbok* adds: 'these things were found in the East on Papey and Papyli.' Both are on the east coast; the first an island, the second a fjord]. It is recorded in English books that at that time there was trafficking between those countries" [Iceland and Britain].

The recollection in Iceland was that Irish religious had lived there before the Norsemen came, in localities in the southeast. The Irish left because of the heathen Norse and left in a hurry, judging by what they left behind. The things that were found are possessions of a monastery and its abbot, perhaps of more than one.

Gaelic place names are found in Iceland, and not only

173

in the southeast. They have been explained as deriving from Norse settlers who came from Ireland or Scotland. Nansen did not think it reasonable that Norsemen would have given Irish names to mountains, streams, and fjords, or to have accepted them from Irish thralls they brought. He concluded that "the most natural explanation is certainly here as with the Faeroes, that there was a primitive Celtic population in Iceland, and not merely a few Irish monks when the Norwegians arrived; and that from these Celts the Icelanders are in part descended, while they took their language from the ruling class, the Norwegians."[10] The survival of Irish place names in various parts of Iceland would seem to imply that some Irish remained after the coming of the Norsemen.

The Irish place names and the remains pertaining to a monastery suggest a colonization by monks and laymen. Monks were in charge; lay help was necessary to get there and sustain the religious. It took competent seamen to cross the long and difficult stretches of ocean. Irish seamen had such experience, learned going to the Hebrides and extended to the Shetlands and Faeroes. The formidable venture north to Iceland was directed by foreknowledge, perhaps by watching the fall migration of birds from the north and their return flights into the north in spring. A familiar theme of Irish legend is the flight of swans, summer inhabitants of Iceland. Once the route was known, communications were continued, as told by Dicuil in the winter voyage and by the reference in the *Landnamabok* to English books that recorded traffic between Britain and Iceland.

A rough calendar may be proposed for the Irish in Iceland and the Faeroes. The Norse settlement of Iceland began about 874, that of the Faeroes at about the same time, according to the Saga of the Faeroes, or a little earlier. The monks left Iceland when the Norse settled. They got out of

---

[10] Nansen, vol. 1, pp. 186–187.

the Faeroes earlier. Dicuil finished his treatise in 825, reporting that the Irish hermits had left the Faeroes because of the viking brigands. Dicuil had been living for a number of years on the continent and wrote what he had heard from a monk who visited the islands. Hermits had lived on them about a hundred years, he wrote, but they were "now vacated by the anchorites." An exodus date around or before 800 seems reasonable. The first serious viking raids against Ireland are recorded in 793, those on the Shetlands and Orkneys perhaps somewhat earlier. The Faeroes, where there was nothing to steal but sheep, may fall into the same period, the hundred years of Irish living in the Faeroes thus considered as the eighth century.

Irish monks reached Iceland before and probably well before the end of the eighth century. Dicuil had his account of the visit by priests some thirty years before he wrote, that is before vikings were harrying the northern coasts of Britain. The priests went on a leisurely visit, starting out in midwinter and therefore knowing that it was a good season to sail north and that they would come to ice free harbors. The inference is that they took a familiar route to Irish establishments in Iceland. Dicuil wrote only about what he heard of the physical geography; the nature of his account is not that of discovery of an unknown land. Lacking better information, we may take a date of entry around 770 at a guess—a hundred years before the Norse.

## BEYOND ICELAND?

By Norse accounts the monks lived in the southeastern part of Iceland. Their departure was hurried but apparently without violence. The Norse chroniclers at least put it gently, saying only that the monks left, not wishing to live beside heathens. As settlers began to come from Norway, the monks and their followers abandoned their abodes and took to the sea.

175

The only direction available lay to the west. Dicuil recorded their knowledge of a frozen sea to the north. The barbarians they feared were coming out of the east. Vikings had been harrying the lands to the south and had begun to live in numbers from the Shetlands to Ireland and also in the way station of the Faeroes. The westward-setting Irminger Current that keeps the south coast of Iceland ice-free would aid them to leave in that direction. And beyond they might find the isles of the blessed long told of in Irish legend. In Iceland the Irish had a hundred years' experience of land, weather, and sea of the far north. They were familiar with navigating the long and hard stretch between the Faeroes and Iceland. As they had once come to discover Iceland, inferring that there was such a land, the time had come again to put themselves to the test of discovery.

Stefansson put it thus: "The New World was discovered by whoever discovered Iceland. For to reach Iceland you must cross a wide and stormy ocean far out of sight of land, while thereafter you can see westward from island to island till the mainland of North America rises above your horizon."[11] The statement is only slightly overdrawn. Continuous sight of land may be had by climbing the proper mountain and having an unusually clear day. Under certain conditions of air inversion distant land may appear in the mirror of mirage.[12] The voyage west from Iceland is much less difficult than getting to Iceland. It could be done as Eric the Red laid it out a century later, west with the Irminger Current, aided by easterly winds in summer, and then southwest to raise Cape Farewell and around it into the sheltered fjords of southwest Greenland. If the Irish made good their escape, it was done in such manner.

The *Islendigabok* reported of Eric's discovery of Green-

[11] Stefansson, vol. 1, p. xi.
[12] Hennig, vol. 2, p. 192.

land: "They found there human habitations, both in the east and the west of the country, also the remains of hide boats and implements of stone, from which it may be seen that men had come of the same kind as inhabit Vinland, whom the Greenlanders call Skraelings." Ari the Learned, who wrote the *Islendigabok*, was a careful chronicler. He composed his book early in the twelfth century, and it is known from copies made in the seventeenth century, which are considered reliable.[13] This is the only mention of Vinland or Skraeling in the book and is considered to be the first notice of both, except for Adam of Bremen's Wineland.

At the time when Eric came and later when Ari wrote, there were no Eskimos or any other natives either in the Eastern or Western Settlement. The archaeology of Greenland has been studied with extraordinary detail and tells of three entries of people out of the Canadian Arctic, all coming into the far northwest of Greenland across Arctic sounds. The first was ancient; the second, known as the Dorset Culture, is dated in the first century A.D. Both disappeared long before Norse time. The third, or Thule Culture, came into northwestern Greenland about the twelfth century, perhaps a century after the Norse had found and settled Greenland.[14] The Thule Eskimos lived as hunters along Arctic shores, where they might be met by an occasional far-ranging Norse hunting party. The *Historia Norvegiae* of about 1170 told of dwarf people called Skraelings thus met to the north, indicating Baffin Bay. In 1267 a Norse party found evidence of Skraelings on Disko Bay, the first record that Eskimos had moved south halfway down the Greenland coast. Their first appearance in the Norse settlements is in the fourteenth century, when the Western Settlement was abandoned.

[13] Jones, p. 224.
[14] Thorkel Matthiasen, *Meddelelser om Grønland*, vol. 161 (Copenhagen, 1958), no. 3.

Eskimos thus are out of the question for the remains that Eric found. Since these were reported both in the Eastern and Western settlements, the chance stranding of a European vessel is out. The finds were noted as habitations and fragments of skin boats, which indicates that they were not very old. What alternative is left other than that the Irish, living there for a time in the ninth century, moved from Eastern to Western Settlement, and then took off across Davis Strait, as the Greenlanders did later? The skin boats then would have been curraghs, replaced here by new ones, made of sealskins, withes, and driftwood, like the ones they had abandoned.

The second part of the statement is in error and seems out of place. It is the only reference to Vinland or Skraelings in the *Islendigabok*. Ari, earliest and most careful of the Icelandic chroniclers, would thus have bypassed both important topics by an erroneous note in the wrong place. There is no lapse into fantasy elsewhere in the chronicle. I suspect it to be an interpolation by a later transcriber, when the Vinland sagas had misappropriated the term Skraeling. Skraeling was still used in the proper sense of dwarf by the *Historia Norvegiae*, a half-century after Ari wrote. The Vinland voyagers found no Eskimos nor did they know native habitations.

## HVITRAMANNALAND, IRELAND THE GREAT

According to the Karlsefni Saga the Norse abandoned Vinland to return to Greenland, sailing with a south wind that gave them opportunity to stop off at Markland. Here the two native boys were taken, to become Christians and learn Norse. Reasons have been given for considering the location to have been Newfoundland, the natives Beothuk Indians, and the time around 1010. The boys told that opposite their own country, on the other side, was another land of different people, where men went about in white dress, shouted loudly, and carried poles with banners. The saga concluded that this must have been Hvitramannaland (White Man's Land) or Ireland the Great, names current at the time for a western land of white men who were thought to be Irishmen. It was held to lie opposite Markland, which would be to the west and indicate a location on the Gulf of St. Lawrence. The *Landnamabok* related of one Ari Marsson:

> He was driven across the sea by heavy gales to Hvitramanna-land, which by some is called Great Ireland. It lies westward in the sea near Vinland the Good. It is said that one can sail thither in six days. Ari could not escape thence and was baptized there. This was first told by Hrafni Hlymreksfari, who had long himself been in Hlymrek in Ireland. Thorkel Gellison [uncle of Ari the Learned] stated also that Icelanders had told, according to what they heard from Thorfinn, Earl of the Orkneys, that Ari [Marsson] had been seen there and recognized in Hvitramanna-land, from which he was not allowed to depart, but that he was otherwise held in great esteem there.[15]

This story was current in Iceland and referred apparently to events of the tenth century, written early in the twelfth. It was told first by a Norseman who had lived in Limerick, and was also heard from the Norse Earl of the Orkneys, both saying in effect that Ari Marsson had been visited by later Norse voyagers to Hvitramannaland. Ari had gone there as a heathen, had been baptized, and remained.

Still another account is in the Eyrbiggja Saga, written down about 1250. Mainly it is the story of one Björn, who left Breidafjord in western Iceland and was carried away in a storm, to be seen later in a western land by another strayed party of Norse, led by a trader named Gudleif who had

---

[15] William Hovgaard, *Voyages of Norsemen into America* (New York, 1914), p. 77.

started out from Dublin. "When he sailed from thence he [Gudleif] was making for Iceland. He sailed to the west of Ireland, encountered there a strong north-east wind, and was driven far to the west and southwest in the ocean until they finally came to a great land which was unknown to them. They did not know the people but thought rather that they spoke Irish." Here they were seized and taken upcountry before an assembly that was to consider their fate. Another band of natives came on horseback, carrying a banner and led by a tall and stately old man, white-haired and of great age. He talked with the captives in Norse, asked in detail about particular persons and places in Iceland, sent presents to those dearest to him, whom he named, and sped the visitors on their way. They thus knew that they had found the missing Björn. Parts of the narrative are reminiscent of Ari Marsson, but all the names are different.[16]

About the time the Vinland story was being written down in Iceland, Icelandic scribes recorded another land in the same direction which they called White Man's Land or Great Ireland. The version of the Skraeling boys came directly to Iceland. The others were relayed from Limerick, the Orkneys, and Dublin, and concern Norsemen who got by accident to a land of white men who were Irish, had been kept there, and were seen later by other Norse parties. The testimony is entirely Norse, and from several independent sources. The *Landnamabok* in particular is carefully factual in identifying its sources. Even in the romantic Eyrbiggja Saga the only absurdity is the party on horseback. It does not seem proper to dismiss Hvitramannaland as fantasy, "entirely mythical" as Jones has termed it, or an "absurdity," according to Oleson. The ever-sceptical Nansen thought that one could hardly accept the Vinland voyages on evidence and deny the reports on Hvitramannaland.

[16] Nansen, vol. 2, pp. 46–48.

An explanation is suggested that accepts the substance of the Norse tales of White Man's Land. The monks and their retinue crossed from Greenland west to Baffin Island and then followed the Canadian shore south along Labrador to the Strait of Belle Isle, turning west there into the Gulf of St. Lawrence. If we accept the remains Eric found in Greenland as left by the Irish, this was the available route of egress. It was thus that Leif later made his discovery of Helluland and Markland, according to the Greenlanders' Saga. In both Vinland sagas the voyagers followed the Atlantic coast. By Norse geography Hvitramannaland was neither Vinland nor Markland but lay on a coast to the west, which indicates the Gulf of St. Lawrence. An approach out of the north would find entry west through the Strait of Belle Isle, opening into a long reach of sea west and southwest and so into the St. Lawrence River. The direction was right by promise of Irish legend that the blessed land lay to the west. At the farther end is the narrowing embayment known as the St. Lawrence River, which opened into an attractive country of hardwoods at the time well populated by Indians.

Norsemen in the British Isles and Iceland believed in and gave evidence of an Irish colony across the sea which had kept to its Christian faith. These Norse tales of ships that strayed from Europe to Hvitramannaland or Great Ireland were not concerned with Vinland. The conversion of Ari Marsson and his detention in the colony refer to the tenth, or the eleventh century. The description by the native boys in Markland, perhaps an Indian version of a Christian religious procession, would indicate that the colony was still in existence when Karlsefni was returning from Vinland early in the eleventh century. There is no incongruity of time nor improbability of route about such Irish settlement. There are too many unconflicting and factual Norse references to such a settlement to be dismissed as fantasy.

181

# NORTHERN MISTS

## *ARCHAEOLOGIC REMAINS?*

A European settlement of medieval age has been excavated lately on Sacred Bay at the entry to the Strait of Belle Isle by Helge and Anne Ingstad.[17] They have presented their remarkable discovery as a Norse village in Vinland.

It is necessary to refer again to the conflicting Vinland Sagas. The Karlsefni Saga minimizes the part of Leif, as storm-driven from Norway to Vinland and puts Karlsefni in charge of the major expedition as the only other one to reach Vinland. Karlsefni is said to have taken the roundabout course from Eastern to Western Settlement and then across Davis Strait to Baffin Island and so south along Canadian shores to winter on Straumfjord, the fjord of the current or stream. Those commentators who follow the Karlsefni Saga have thought to identify this fjord with the Strait of Belle Isle.[18] The Greenlanders' Saga, it is important to recall, does not mention Straumfjord or a coastwise approach from the north subsequent to Leif's voyage.

The bleak and windswept Strait of Belle Isle (through which I once passed in early July) bears no resemblance to the gracious country of deciduous woodlands and grape-vines of Vinland, bordered by wide tidal flats. Ingstad therefore accepted the archaic word *vin* as meaning grass instead of grapes. The Straumfjord identification, if there was indeed such a place, has remained puzzling. The Scots pair brought grapes and self-sown wheat from the north of Straumfjord. After the hard winter at Straumfjord Karlsefni sent one party north to look for Vinland while he took the main party far south in its search.

One of the most important discoveries of the Ingstad

---

[17] Helge and Anne Ingstad, preliminary account in *National Geographic* (November 1964).
[18] Jones, pp. 220–223.

excavation was the local smelting of iron. The ore used was bog limonite of algal origin, such as later supplied the early iron industry of New England. Bog iron was of major importance during the Middle Ages in northwestern Europe, including Norway and Ireland. The settlements in Iceland and Greenland depended on fabricated iron imported from Norway, perhaps the major necessity they needed to purchase and apparently always in short supply. Greenland archaeologists have watched closely for evidence of local iron making.[19] The results have been meager. Occasional bits of slag have been found, some of bog iron, others of magnetite, and it has been debated whether they were of local origin or might have been introduced accidentally. Several smithies have been found, and some indication of smelting in a small way. If iron was produced during the long life of the Greenland settlements, it was very little and exceptional.

At the Belle Isle site, slag of bog iron was soon found and shortly a "smithy" with "a bonanza: hundreds of pieces of slag" weighing about thirty pounds, with small bits of iron and bog iron ore. The expertness needed to reduce bog limonite to iron was employed here promptly. It is strange that the Vinland accounts that told so much of what happened in Vinland should have said nothing of something so important and uncommon. Charcoal taken from the ancient village has provided radiocarbon dates, only one, according to the published account, as late as the time of the Vinland voyages. The explanation given is that old driftwood was used, which recorded the time of the living tree.

Identification of the Belle Isle village as Norse is somewhat less than convincing as to place or time. It makes sense as passage into the Gulf of St. Lawrence, which the Vinland farers did not enter. The Greenland Saga has no place in its

---

[19] In particular Niels Nielsen in the *Meddelelser om Grønland*, e.g., vols. 76 and 88.

clearly consecutive account for such a locality. On the other hand the site was the northern gateway into the Gulf of St. Lawrence through which the Irish would have passed on their way south to Hvitramannaland, if there was such a country, as is supported by diverse Norse testimony. If this thesis is accepted the Belle Isle site fits properly into the Irish exodus, from Iceland to Greenland to the Strait of Belle Isle and so to the St. Lawrence. The foundations of the structures are as proper to Irish builders as to Norse. And the working of iron was a Celtic specialty. In the early Middle Ages the Irish mined copper and gold and dug bog iron ore in Ireland and were superior workers of metals. Their monasteries held artisans of diverse skills, nor is it likely that these were omitted from the parties that went to remote parts. As they went north from the homeland with experienced sailors and boat builders, so they should have taken with them persons knowledgeable of smithing and founding. A temporary settlement on the Strait of Belle Isle would have given opportunity to reconnoiter the way west, mend their boats, and supply their needs of iron, depleted by living in Iceland and Greenland. They could provision themselves at Belle Isle before they sought a better land to the west.

## CONTACT WITH INDIANS?

The thesis that there was a Christian and Irish colony overseas on the St. Lawrence Gulf or River gains credibility from the manner in which it was referred to in different Norse texts, casually as a matter generally known might be. With the exception of the two boys Karlsefni caught, the episodes have nothing to do with the Vinland voyages. They tell of individual Norsemen, who are named, living in an Irish–Indian country, where they are visited by other named Norsemen. The implication is that during the tenth century, before Vinland, perhaps before the Norse settlement of

Greenland, Norsemen had repeatedly strayed across the Atlantic and got to Hvitramannaland. The story Karlsefni later got from the Indian boys in Markland may refer to a ceremonial in the Christian manner that was continued after the lifetime of the monks.

Historically the country in question was occupied by Algonquian tribes, except for the Iroquois whom Cartier found in the St. Lawrence Valley. In Vinland the Norsemen turned the natives hostile by senseless killings. At later times Europeans, French, English, and Dutch were received hospitably in Algonquian settlements. Such was indeed almost always the case in the New World and continued to be true until the natives were abused and dispossessed. The Irish monks and their followers would have come and remained in peace as they carried a Christianizing mission. Centuries later the French missionaries were able to do so everywhere, even among the Iroquois, except when French arms were used against natives, as Champlain foolishly did, thereby beginning the long and fateful Iroquois hostility.

The several attempts to find Norse elements in Indian cultures of the Northeast have failed, as might be expected considering the briefness and antagonism of the contacts. The possibility of an Irish linkage has not been considered seriously. Early French missionaries in Canada were worried by what seemed to them perversions or vestiges of Christianity. Was the Devil mocking them when they found the cross associated with the service of manito, and also used as a design on the body and in crafts? At the great Indian winter ceremonial of the year, strangely resembling Passion Week, a chosen dog was hanged on a cross-like structure, taken down after a time, and carried by mourning procession to burial. The great collective rite was performed annually, it seems, from the St. Lawrence to the western Great Lakes. Lewis Morgan witnessed such a ceremony and gave a good description of it in his *League of the Iroquois*. The strange sacrifice has a non-Indian quality that asks for study. Henry Rand Schoolcraft spent many years learning the traditions and customs of western Algonquian tribes, and his observations gave Longfellow the material for *Hiawatha*. Indian religions, like other parts of Indian cultures, commonly are considered as having developed *in situ*. The possibility of diffusion of cultural traits, especially from distant parts overseas, has largely been shunned in American Indian studies. Were the French missionaries in Canada confronted by distorted remnants of the teachings of earlier Christian missionaries, an Irish colony gradually absorbed into Indian culture, as the last Norse were into Eskimo?

# CHAPTER IX DARK AGES
# AND TENEBROUS SEA?

*THE CELTIC SEA FRINGE*

Celtic peoples held the continental shores between Flanders and the Pyrenees and also the British Isles until brought under Roman rule. Ireland and highland Scotland were never invaded by Roman arms, and only part of Wales. About the Irish Sea a Celtic culture continued in vigor, accepting the Christian faith freely, happily, and in its own manner. For more than three centuries this Celtic Christianity retained its particular character, which was monastic rather than episcopal. Monks went out, as "families" and singly, to be missionaries, found monasteries, go as *peregrini* into far places, withdraw into hermitages. The early Irish and Welsh saints lived out their lives recognized as holy men without the seal of martyrdom. Nor were the monks organized into one order governed and bound by common observance. Irish monks were distinguished by their learning and inquiry. St. Vergilius supported the idea of a spherical Earth against English St. Boniface. Dicuil entitled his book *The measure of the earth's orb*. Ireland of the early Middle Ages was the most enlightened land of the West.

However illegible the facts are in the Irish sea legends, the Irish looked to the sea for adventure and discovery in praise of God, not in fear of mishap and danger nor for gain. A persistent theme is that the land of the blessed, called the Isle of Brasil, lay in the ocean to the west. St. Brendan, whose legend tells of years of romantic sailing, was a real abbot of

187

known parts who did go to sea. St. Columba built the monastery on the sacred isle of Iona and from there undertook conversion and colonization that carried through the Hebrides into the Orkneys. By the seventh century the Shetlands were Irish Christian well before the islands were reached and named by Norsemen. Mainly by curragh, Irish seamen went far into unknown seas and uninhabited islands. Early in the ninth century the Irish monk Dicuil wrote at the Frankish court the first account of the Faeroe Islands and of Iceland, in both of which Irish monks had settled a century or so earlier.

The later accounts of Irish seafaring were told by the Norse. When these came to Iceland they found Irish priests there, who left as the heathen Norse took up their homesteads. When Eric the Red explored Greenland he found the remains of houses and boats in an unpeopled land, long before Eskimos began to enter Greenland. I know no other explanation than that the Irish who had left Iceland stopped there on their way west, the only direction open to them and the one blessed in their legends. Later the Norse knew, from independent sources in Iceland and the British Isles, of a Hvitramannaland or Great Ireland to the west across the farther ocean. These stories were given with details of persons and places that cannot be dismissed as mere fantasy. The indicated location is on the Gulf of St. Lawrence and the time the tenth century, before that of the Vinland voyages.

## VIKING SEAFARING

In Norse saga and chronicle viking was an occupational name, applied to a person who had gone to sea and gained distinction by fighting and plundering in foreign parts. The motives were in extreme contrast to Celtic seafaring. The Norse gained prestige by violence of conduct, by hardihood in war, and by success in looting. The very figureheads of viking ships declared that they came to bring terror. Their preferred attack was by surprise and was directed against places where there was wealth, especially treasure, to be taken and carried off.

Heavy viking raids extended to Ireland by the end of the eighth century, despoiling castles and monasteries, and shortly driving the unarmed Irish boats from the sea. Vikings set themselves up as lords over the northern islands from the Shetlands to the Hebrides and began piecemeal the conquest of Ireland, which was about half completed before Irish chieftains rallied to successful counterattack late in the ninth century. Ireland was thus saved from becoming a land of Norse principalities and remained Christian, but never regained its seafaring ways.

The wild, free viking time began to break down during the ninth century, in part because the Norse in the British Isles were on a losing defensive, and largely because King Harald Fair Hair brought the vikings in Norway forcibly to heel. Erstwhile vikings in numbers then set out to find new homes in the Faeroes and Iceland, there to become stockmen and fishermen. Iceland was fully settled in sixty years and a generation later experienced its first famine. Eric the Red led a party of land seekers to Greenland in 986 and from here, in or shortly after the year 1000, a last brief search for new land was made by the Vinland voyagers. The descendants of vikings had become modest homesteaders, making out on the narrow resources of Iceland and Greenland and relinquishing the greater attractions of Vinland after they had stirred up the enmity of the natives. Having established themselves by way stations across the North Atlantic, they failed to take hold at the farther and more promising end. Nansen noted that Ari the Learned, the ablest Icelandic chronicler, gave Vinland passing mention, less than he did to Hvitramannaland. By the mid-thirteenth century Greenland was rarely visited by ships and Norwegian seafaring had declined to the extent that most of its com-

merce was in other hands. Viking venturesomeness was long
gone by then, having passed in the tenth century.

## IN THE HIGH MIDDLE AGES

Of the four hundred years between the Vinland voyages
and the time of Prince Henry nothing that is sure and little
that is credible was added to geographic knowledge of the
northern Atlantic. However, commerce on the high sea increased greatly, mainly between north and south Europe.
At the north Hanseatic merchants organized the water-
borne trade of the Baltic, North, and Norwegian seas. When
there was prospect of cargo they sent as far as Iceland. Broad-
bellied cargo ships gave larger carrying capacity, A major
herring fishery developed about the northern seas. Its processed products, along with salt, wool, hides, lumber, and
pitch provided bulk cargoes for a large merchant fleet. The
cities of Flanders became the main meeting place of sea-
borne commerce between north and south.

To the south Basques and their Asturian neighbors
turned to seafaring and trading, and Basques made a particular business of following the great right whales north from
their wintering grounds in the Bay of Biscay. They introduced dried and salt cod, known as bacalao, as a staple in
Mediterranean markets, as the Hanse did for herring north
of the Alps. Cod, caught by hook and line, were taken from
the Bay of Biscay northward in about the same waters as
were the right whales. Basque shipwrights fashioned a seaworthy cargo ship of their own, Englished as balinger, so
named from its first use in whaling. Basques and Asturians
joined in a powerful seafaring league, the Hermandad de las
Marismas, which gave principal naval support to France in
the Hundred Years' War and entered into treaties of truce
with the English Crown.

As far out as the Northern Atlantic was of interest to

190

commerce, its waters were ranged freely by ships of various nations throughout the high Middle Ages, going by direct routes to destinations across the seas.

## PRINCE HENRY AND SUCCESSORS

Portugal was late in turning to the high seas, but did so with rapid and great success in the fifteenth century. Prince Henry instructed and financed navigation, planned and planted overseas colonies and factories, and charted far sea routes. At his death in 1460 the Portuguese advance had reached south along Africa to the Gulf of Guinea and west to the Azores Islands, secure bases for the spectacular results of his successors. The opening of the route to the Indies around Africa made Portugal the first world power. That Prince Henry gave persistent attention to the west has been less noted by scholars.

The Azores, according to the record, were not discovered by the chance of a storm-driven ship but by search of the western ocean. Prince Henry then took ample time to populate the islands with livestock before he began to plant settlers, first Portuguese, then Flemings in such numbers that the islands were also known as the Flemish Isles. Thus he established in mid-ocean a usable and permanent base for farther exploration west and, later, northwest. The Azores were so used to the beginning of the sixteenth century. Portugal had in mind the alternative possibility of sailing west to the Far East. That this was in the mind of Prince Henry is inferred from his assemblage of astronomers and persons learned in cosmology and cartography, men who had knowledge of the shape, perhaps also of the size, of the Earth. Ten years or so after the death of Prince Henry, his nephew King Alfonso asked Toscanelli in Florence what he thought about sailing west to the Indies. At the time the African voyages were discouraging, each bringing word of

191

a farther southward extension of the land. Alfonso, taught by his uncle, we may infer, recalled what he had been told of the alternative route west.

The base Henry had prepared with care in the Azores was used from mid-century to reconnoiter the sea to the west. Men were given patents to discover and possess at their own expense. At about the same time as the Toscanelli inquiry Alfonso corresponded with the king of Denmark concerning an exploration into the northwest and sent João Vaz Corte Real to accompany the Danish expedition that was led by the captains Pining and Pothorst. By one view this was for the "rediscovery" of Greenland, which in fact was not unknown nor was it as yet completely abandoned by the Greenlanders. The likelier view, presented by Sophus Larsen, is that it extended to American shores.

The Azores continued to serve as starting place for western discovery, indeed may have seen the beginning of the search for a northwest passage. From 1500 the sons of the elder Corte Real—the family being the leading gentry of the Azores—went on expeditions to Newfoundland and adjacent parts, which was thereby known as the land of Corte Real or Bacalhaos. Another Azorian gave his name to Labrador, probably by way of Bristol. The Azores, lying midway between Portugal and Newfoundland and its Grand Banks, have continued to the present to link Portugal and northeastern America.

## BRISTOL SHIPS IN THE NORTHERN ATLANTIC

The Bristol voyages across the Atlantic about 1480 were preceded by years of far-ranging sea traffic, both north and south. Early in the century Bristol merchants brought salt fish from Iceland. When Madeira was planted, Bristol ships carried its wine and sugar to England. Bristol seamen

were familiar with the ports of Portuguese mainland and islands. Portuguese came to live in Bristol. The tradition of a
western land or island of the Seven Cities, long current in
Portugal and Spain, was transplanted to Bristol. The Irish
legend of a western island of Brasil was added to that of the
Seven Cities, both to be the object of search. Thus men of
Bristol found the prime cod fishing grounds on Canadian
shores and perhaps learned to appreciate the fine pelts the
Indians prepared. It is known that their voyages to western
lands began about ten years before Columbus and that they
were repeated, but little more. The merchants of Bristol were
not interested in advertising what they had found across the
sea. The beginnings of cod fishing on western shores, as for
instance the date when Bretons began to participate, are
still uncertain.

The role of John Cabot in discovery has been clarified
and somewhat reduced. His arrival in England with his family
was probably in 1495. He may have been for a while before
then in Spain. He came to England to promote a sea route
west to the spice lands and addressed himself to merchants of
Bristol for ships and crew and to the king for the patent. It
has been thought that the idea was new to England, which
would be rather curious, with the familiar contacts Bristol
had maintained with island and mainland Portuguese. As
with Columbus, it is not of record that Cabot had experience
as a navigator. He must have been a remarkable salesman,
getting both the means from the merchants and the patent
from the king, and in so short a time. That he went promptly
to Bristol suggests that he knew Bristol could furnish the
men experienced in crossing the western sea. He knew of
the discovery of Columbus and of the succeeding disappointment of Spain. It was Cabot's shrewd plan that the English
Crown could be interested in another route to the spice lands

if backing and men were provided from Bristol. And thus he took his project to England and promoted it to early acceptance.

It is now known that Cabot made a trial voyage from Bristol in 1496 which was unsuccessful. The following year he set out again in a small ship, manned by a small crew and carrying at least two merchants from Bristol. The crossing was made in about five weeks, the party landing for a few hours, to go through the ritual of taking possession for England. They filled their water casks and sailed for a month along the coast, seeing no one nor landing again. Where they landed is unknown. The clues do not point to Newfoundland, as tradition would have it, but to a shore farther west, perhaps as far as New England. As the territorial game was played by European powers, the manner of landing gave title to England and glory to John Cabot, who did not know where he was and got there by a Bristol ship managed by Bristol seamen, who had been to such shores before. There is a monument to Cabot in England, but none I believe to its people, who made the voyage possible and knew the way. History does not celebrate the anonymous.

During the whole of the Middle Ages peoples of Atlantic Europe went to sea according to their particular interests. The Irish were first and they went out widely as missionaries, pilgrims, and hermits to be first to settle Faeroes and Iceland and, by slender but consistent evidence, to be the first Europeans to reach and remain on the North American mainland. What lay beyond the known horizon attracted them as pious romantics. The Norse sagas on the other hand stress discoveries by accident, of ships that were driven off course. Viking seafaring rested on a cult of daring and violence bringing prestige with plunder and conquest. It dominated the seas for two centuries and drove the Irish permanently from the seas. Except for Vinland, the Norse followed, mainly or entirely, routes of Irish discovery. As viking ways were lost the Norse changed to the humble satisfactions of taking homesteads in the Faeroes, Iceland, and Greenland, with a brief and weak venture to Vinland.

The high Middle Ages added no verified northern discoveries. They were, however, a time of increased maritime activity and competence. In the north the Hanseatic League, and on the Bay of Biscay the Hermandad de las Marismas, in effect were sovereign powers, operating naval as well as merchant ships. The North Atlantic herring, bacalao, and right whale production, processing, and distribution supplied European markets widely and in quantity. Capacious and seaworthy cargo ships were developed and were manned by seamen who knew the high northern seas, celestial navigation, and the compass.

The familiar story how Prince Henry led Portugal to exploration and colonization overseas gives main attention to the route around Africa. His interest and planning was also directed to the west, as shown by the discovery of the Azores, the careful preparations for their settlement, the manner of their settlement, and their use as a base for farther exploration. That he and the group of scholars about him knew the Earth as a globe, as the Irish monks had long before, is accepted. This knowledge is also implicit in the inquiry his nephew Alfonso later made of Toscanelli, to be heard of later by Columbus. The Azores ultimately served in the discovery of American lands to the northwest by Azorians of the Corte Real family and the man called Labrador. It was, however, men of Bristol, familiar with the Azores, Madeira, and mainland Portugal, who seem to have come first to the ill-defined "new found land."

Shortly afterwards the Grand Banks of Newfoundland were visited and shared amicably by fishermen of a half dozen nationalities, coming and returning year after year, living at sea for months at a stretch. This was their accustomed and experienced way of life, including hazard and discomfort. Their kin and kindred went not as men against a hostile sea from which they hoped to escape but following the livelihood at which they were competent.

The seafarers into the northern mists did so for the thousand years of the Middle Ages, for spiritual adventure, for refuge from world or king, to find homesteads, to profit by commerce, whatever drove or drew them to what might lie beyond the horizon.

# INDEX

197

# INDEX

198

# INDEX